Tab

Introduction vii

Chapter 1 — Gainsharing Philosophy: A System of Management or a Compensation Plan? 1

Chapter 2 — The Gainsharing Foundation: Four Key Principles 9
- Figure 1: Four Key, Interrelated Principles of Gainsharing 11
- Equity 10
- Identity 12
- Involvement/Participation 13
- Figure 2: Comparison of Pre- and Post-Gainsharing Survey 14
- Figure 3: Comparison of Pre- and Post-Gainsharing Survey 15
- Commitment 16
- Figure 4: Comparison of Pre- and Post-Gainsharing Survey 19

Chapter 3 — The Calculation Philosophy: Control or Common-Fate Orientation 21
- Figure 5: Gainsharing Plan Purpose Statements 23
- Physical vs. Financial Measures 23
- Figure 6: The Dichotomy Between Physical and Financial Measures 24
- Figure 7: Common-Fate Orientation 25
- Figure 8A: Bonus Calculations As Related to Physical Measure and Minor Level of Employee Involvement 26
- Figure 8B: Bonus Calculations As Related to Physical Measure and Moderate Level of Employee Involvement 27
- Figure 8C: Bonus Calculations As Related to Financial Measure and High Level of Employee Involvement 27
- Figure 8D: Bonus Calculations As Related to Financial Measure and Minor Level of Employee Involvement 27
- Employee Involvement — Minor vs. Major 28
- Operating Performance vs. Profits 30
- Figure 9: Operating Performance & Profits Matrix 31

Chapter 4 — The Distribution Group: Boundaries 35
- Figure 10: Line of Sight for a Worker on Piecework 37
- Gainsharing Implementation Case Study 37
- Figure 11: Distribution Alternatives 38
- Broad Measurement — Common Distribution Group 38

- Figure 12, Model 1: Broad Measure, Common Group 39
- Figure 13: Line of Sight for Broad Measure, Common Group 39
- Narrow Measures, Common Group 40
- Figure 14, Model 2: Narrow Measures, Common Group 40
- Figure 15: Line of Sight for Narrow Measures, Common Group 41
- Narrow Measures, Independent Group 41
- Figure 16, Model 3: Narrow Measures, Independent Group 42
- Figure 17: Line of Sight for Narrow Measures, Independent Group 42
- Narrow Measures, Blended Group 43
- Figure 18, Model 4: Narrow Measures, Blended Group 43
- Figure 19: Line of Sight for Narrow Measures, Blended Group 44
- Factors to Consider — Defining the Group 45
- Interdependence..45
- Administration 46
- Influence..46
- Identity 46
- Inequities 46

Chapter 5 — Measurement 49
- Figure 20: Multicost Single Ratio..51
- Figure 21: Family of Measures Model 52
- Figure 22: Pool Accumulation...53
- Advantages of the Family of Measures Approach 54
- Figure 23: Family of Measures Example...56
- Measurement Criteria 58
- Figure 24: Criteria Screening Tool..58
- Figure 25: "Trigger" or "Gate" Measure 61

Chapter 6 — Calculation Issues: Values, Sharing and Gatekeepers...............65
- Valuing the Gain 66
- Figure 26: Multicost Gain 66
- Figure 27: Allowable Hours Formula 67
- Figure 28: Units per Payroll Hour Formula 68
- Figure 29: Value per Unit..68
- Sharing the Gains..69
- Appropriate Level of Award for Appropriate Level of Performance 70
- Figure 30: Standard Bonus Scale 70
- Figure 31: Comparison of Two Facilities...71
- Gatekeeper Measures 73

Chapter 7 — Baseline Consideration: Setting the Bar 75
- History 76
- Figure 32: Using Historical Data as a Baseline 77
- Target as the Baseline...78
- Figure 33: Rolling Average 79
- Figure 34: Variable Share Approach 79
- Baseline Adjustments..80
- Figure 35: Effects of a Fixed Baseline 81
- Figure 36: Fixed vs. Rachet Baseline 82
- Figure 37: Baseline Adjustments...83
- Figure 38: Baseline Adjustments
  with Less Aggressive Weighted Averaging Approach 84
- Mid-Year Baseline Adjustments...85

Chapter 8 — Frequency of Payout, Minimum Payout and Reserve Account Frequency 89
- Minimum Payout 90
- The Reserve Account 91
- Figure 39: Effect of Variability 91
- Figure 40: Deficit Reserve 92
- Figure 41: Deficit Reserve...94

Chapter 9 — Method of Distribution.................................95
- Equal Share..96
- Figure 42: Methods of Distribution 97
- Equal Percent 99
- Equal Cents per Hour 99
- Split Distribution 99
- Figure 43: Split Distribution 100

Chapter 10 — Other Plan Policies 101
- Eligibility..102
- Termination Policies 102
- Plan Year 103
- Communications 103
- Employee Involvement 103

Chapter 11 — The Design Team and Implementation Steps 105
- Why a Design Team? 106
- Design Team's Role 107
- Who's on the Team? 108
- Criteria for Choosing a Design Team Member 108
- Parameters for Team's Decision-making 109
- Implementation Steps 109
- Figure 44: Plan Components 110
- Sidebar: A Word of Caution 111
- Figure 45: Typical Flow of the Implementation Process 112
- Step 1: Education/Orientation of Management Staff 112
- Readiness Assessment Checklist 113
- Step 2: Purpose and Goals 114
- Step 3: Employee Awareness 114
- Step 4: Model Development, Measures and Simulations 115
- Step 5: Design Team Formal Plan Development Phase 116
- Step 6: Plan Kickoff 116
- Step 7: Implementation/Training 117
- Involvement Training 117
- General Employee Training and Communication 117
- Plan Coordinator 117
- Step 8: Monitoring Phase 118
- Figure 46: Implementation Plan Timeline 119

Chapter 12 — The Employee Involvement System 121
- Involvement Teams 123
- The Review Board 123
- Figure 47: Idea Flow 124

Chapter 13 — End Results 127
- Actual Results 129
- Figure 48: Positive Results from Gainsharing 129
- Figure 49: Three-Month Rolling Average Productivity 130
- Figure 50: Molding Operations, First-Year Plan Results 131
- Figure 51: Metal Extrusion Operation, First-Year Plan Results .. 132
- Figure 52: Survey Comparison One Year After Implementation 133
- A Process to Develop Human Assets 133

Selected References 137

Introduction

Gainsharing, very simply, is "employee involvement with teeth." Moreover, gainsharing is a tool that drives organizational change. This book focuses on the gainsharing philosophy, as well as its technical and social considerations.

Chapters 1 and 2 focus on the gainsharing theory and conceptual issues including the key foundations of gainsharing: equity, identity, involvement and commitment. As with a physical structure, the development of a strong foundation will ensure a viable plan that will stand the test of time. Too many gainsharing plan failures have been caused by a lack of top-management understanding of the concepts and the commitment that is required. Without full-management understanding and endorsement of the key gainsharing principles, the plan will struggle or perhaps fail. The reader will learn that gainsharing is not merely an incentive but more of a system or philosophy of managing.

In Chapter 3 the control versus common-fate measurement philosophies are explored. The reader also will learn that the appropriate measurements need to be aligned with the culture of the workplace. The current level of trust, involvement and information sharing will have a dramatic influence on the plan's design and success.

Chapter 4 raises the critical question of determining the boundaries for gainsharing, such as what is the group that will share in the gains, and what are the boundaries for participation? Various models are reviewed and issues to consider are discussed.

Chapter 5 reviews plan measures. Technical considerations/issues will focus on measurement systems used to calculate gains. Obviously the measures must support the business. Therefore, one plan does not suit all. A method for rating potential measures is presented. The need for the measurement system to evolve over time also is discussed.

Chapters 6 to 10 review gainsharing plan components. A host of issues needs to be addressed before a plan is implemented. Examples and arguments for different plan alternatives are presented.

Chapter 11 covers the implementation process and provides an example of an organization's timeline. The role of employees' involvement in the plan's development is stressed.

The engine for gainsharing, employee involvement, is discussed in Chapter 12. Chapter 13 shares some case study results achieved by organizations and identifies critical factors for success.

It is our hope that after reading this book, you will have a better understanding of the gainsharing philosophy and an appreciation for the level of commitment required to implement and maintain a successful plan.

1

Gainsharing Philosophy: A System of Management or a Compensation Plan?

I was recently traveling to St. Louis, and I overheard some passengers across the aisle discussing human resources issues. The discussion caught my attention, and I asked my neighbors if they worked in the field. They responded, "Yes, in a way. We are benefits consultants." I responded, "Then you must know about my field. I'm a gainsharing consultant." Their response was, "Oh, isn't that like profit sharing?"

If you are a compensation professional, you undoubtedly know that gainsharing is not profit sharing. However, fundamentally, many people have a misunderstanding of what gainsharing truly is, even some who have a plan in place. One of the more common views is that gainsharing is a compensation or group incentive plan.

Experience has taught me that gainsharing is much more than a compensation plan; it has a much broader meaning. Interestingly, those who have the opportunity to be associated with a successful plan may see gainsharing as a "quality of work life" initiative. Some refer to gainsharing as an "employee involvement system with teeth," while others see the concept as a system or tool to drive organizational (cultural) change.

The term "gainsharing" should be taken literally. As an organization gains, it shares. The typical gainsharing organization measures performance and through a predetermined formula, shares the productivity gains with all employees. The organization's actual performance is compared to baseline performance (typically a historical standard) to determine the amount of the gain. Since gains are measured in relationship to a historical baseline, employees and the organization need to change to generate a gain.

The following statements typically apply to and are present in a gainsharing plan:

- Gains and resulting payouts are self-funded.
- The plan commonly applies to a single plant, site or stand-alone

organization. However, some organizations have levels of sharing across multiple locations or corporationwide.

- Performance typically is measured across departments/units/functions.
- Measures commonly are narrower and controllable by employees rather than an organizationwide measure of profits. However, some organizations have measures as broad as profits.
- Payout often is monthly or quarterly.
- Many plans have a year-end reserve fund to account for deficit periods.
- Employees often are involved with the design process.
- All employees are eligible for plan payments.
- The bonus often is paid as an equal percentage of compensation or equal cents per hour worked, rather than paid on the basis of individual performance.
- A supporting employee involvement system is part of the plan to drive improvement initiatives.

At the basic level, gainsharing appears to be a group incentive or compensation system. However, to appreciate the gainsharing concept, one should understand gainsharing's roots and underlying principles. A definition of the term is a good place to start.

> **Gainsharing** may be best described as a system or philosophy of management that promotes higher levels of organizational performance through the involvement and participation of its people. As performance improves, employees share financially in the gain.
>
> Gainsharing is a team approach that emphasizes cooperation and working smarter. Generally, all employees at a site or operation are included.

The gainsharing concept's roots date back to the 1930s when Joe Scanlon, a labor leader, preached that "the worker" had much more to offer than a pair of hands. In effect, the person closest to the problem often has the best and simplest solution. Moreover, if the worker is involved in the solution, he or she most likely will make the solution work.

After the Depression, Scanlon's employer emerged from bankruptcy with obsolete equipment and high costs. Wages were low, and as the company entered labor negotiations, the union submitted demands for higher pay and improved working conditions. If the demands were granted, the company's survival would be seriously threatened. Scanlon took the company president to the union headquarters in Pittsburgh to discuss the problems. At the urging of the International Union, the parties returned to the mill and interviewed every employee to explain the dilemma and enlist each person's support to reduce waste and cost to assure the company's survival. The immediate wage demands were tabled, and within months, the joint labor-management efforts resulted in significant cost reductions and quality improvements. As the company made progress, it was able to grant a wage increase and improve conditions of employment. In the spirit of continued labor-management cooperation, employee teams were formed to review productivity improvement ideas.

Obviously, the labor-management cooperation effort was not easy. It took a lot of hard work and commitment. The Scanlon Plan became known as "a frontier in labor-management cooperation." Scanlon went on to work at MIT to help other labor leaders and managers. The point is that the Scanlon Plan was an employee involvement initiative rather than a compensation/incentive plan. Many employee involvement systems today have their fundamental roots from Scanlon.

If Scanlon were alive now he very likely would say that gainsharing is a philosophy of managing, "the creation philosophy" rather than a "compensation plan." Unfortunately, traditional compensation is based on the "exchange theory" of compensation. Conversely, gainsharing supports the creation philosophy, which says that as we create improved performance, all employees share financially and in many other ways.

The traditional exchange approach says, "If you do this, you will get paid that." In the traditional sense, pay is used as a form of management control. Employees are to perform specific functions and in return are paid for their time. Companies have elaborate systems for evaluating jobs and go to great lengths to maintain the system. This approach, however, reinforces behavior that limits flexibility. What are the chances that an employee will go beyond his/her normal job boundaries? An employee asks, "Why should I take on more responsibility? It's not my job and I won't get paid for the effort."

Also, the exchange approach, which attempts to recognize individual performance, has been a significant failure. Individual performance is very difficult to measure in a fair and objective manner. Companies have been searching for the perfect performance evaluation system for years. Many studies support the fact that too often employees do not believe that they will personally benefit if they are more effective on their job.

Finally, the exchange theory fosters an environment of individual competition often in conflict with the need for more employee collaboration and cooperation.

I personally can relate to the exchange theory vs. the creation philosophy. I grew up on a farm in Michigan and never received an allowance while growing up. I was expected to help with whatever needed to be done as my contribution to the family.

As my wife and I started our own family, we decided not to pay our children an allowance. However, our neighbors took another approach. They paid their children a weekly allowance, feeling it taught them responsibility and money management. In "exchange" for the allowance, the children were expected to perform some typical household duties. For example, Jimmy received $5 a week to keep his room clean, $1 to wash the dishes and $2 to wash the car. Because the lawn was a much bigger job, Jimmy received $10. However, the lawn work also required the final step of trimming the fencerow with the weed-eater. After he finished the lawn, Jimmy was eager to be paid the $10. Sometimes the job was not the best, and Jimmy was required to go back and do some extra weed-eating. Sometimes if Jimmy pestered them enough, his parents paid him the $10 even though the job was not totally satisfactory. On Friday at the dinner table the family would discuss weekend plans. One time Jimmy's dad suggested that they get up early on Saturday morning and clean the basement. Jimmy's response, "How much?" The inevitable had happened; Jimmy was conditioned by the exchange theory of compensation.

Today's focus is on quality and customer satisfaction. Employee teamwork and collaboration are essential to accomplish these and other goals. Gainsharing is a nontraditional, team-based approach. Instead of focusing on the exchange theory, gainsharing builds on teamwork, collaboration and working smarter. Employees, departments and the total organization work together to "create" improved performance by focusing on common goals. The concept says, "We are in this together; let's just do it! Together we create improved performance, and as performance improves, we will all share in the gain." However, rather than the payment being the primary focus, it becomes almost a byproduct of the organization's culture. There are a number of nonmonetary gains: the sense of self-confidence, ownership, teamwork, pride and feeling of control. A great deal of employee identity to the organization and its goals are developed.

As I explained earlier, I was raised on a farm and didn't receive an allowance while growing up. I was raised under the creation philosophy. I'll never forget my summer job the year I was nine. I was to paint the white fence surrounding a five-acre field. I didn't get paid a nickel for the job. It took me all summer, and I spilled a lot of paint. At the time, our farm was relatively small, about 100 acres. The next summer, with my painting skills refined, I was ready to tackle the barns. When I was 11, I painted the house, an even bigger challenge, and the quality of work was essential. When I was 12, we purchased another farm about one mile from the homestead. The following year, we purchased a third farm that adjoined the homestead. I can remember that we leveraged our real estate and fell further in debt. When I was 16, the farm was prosperous and had grown to well over 400 acres. By that time, I was not only painting but also tilling fields, feeding cattle and harvesting apples. We invested long hours of sweat and toil into the land. Of course, I never received an allowance or compensation for my time. I vividly remember often going out on Saturday nights to the movies with my friends. We had a cigar box in the kitchen. The box held the money from our cash crops. Before leaving for the evening, I would take cash from the "money box" to cover the movie ticket. My dad would often ask if I had enough money. He would say, "Take an extra $10. You don't want to be caught short. There is plenty there right now." When I returned late in the evening from my Saturday outing, I would go to the money box and put back $11 in change. Do you think my dad trusted me? Of course he did. Did I trust my dad? I sure did. Whose farm is it? If you respond, "the family's," you're right. It's my mother's, my father's and my two brothers', as well as mine. Who created the farm? We did. Do I have pride in the farm? You better believe it. Who's created your organization? Doesn't it make sense to share?

The creation philosophy doesn't happen overnight, but many organizations make the shift. Gainsharing is for the long term. It doesn't fit organizations that are looking for a quick fix. A great deal of management commitment is required, including communicating performance, training and fostering an environment that supports employee involvement. Management needs to be open to listening to employee ideas and concerns.

2

The Gainsharing Foundation: Four Key Principles

There are four relatively simple principles that should help you understand why gainsharing works. These principles may not be complicated, but they are powerful. All four principles are incorporated in the strategy used to install and maintain a successful plan. I can't claim ownership of these principles. They were developed and refined by one of the original disciples of Joe Scanlon. These principles have been preached by some of the best employers in North America. Organizations like Wescast Industries, Magna Donnelly, Beth Israel Hospital, Dana, Herman Miller and Motorola were all ranked in the Top 50 Best Places to work when their Scanlon plans were active.

Today many organizations continue to practice these principles. In fact, some of these organizations participate in the Scanlon Network, an association of companies with the same values. The principles run counter to many organizational behaviors that lead to corporate scandals and unethical practices. The four principles address:

- Equity
- Identity
- Involvement
- Commitment.

The four principles are interrelated and mutually reinforcing. (See Figure 1 on page 11.)

A partial description of these principles can help the reader develop a better understanding of the foundation for gainsharing.

Equity

The equity principle is based on the philosophy that it's fair to share. Everyone in the organization makes a contribution to the institution's success. Why limit bonuses to the select few? People typically take pride in their work and

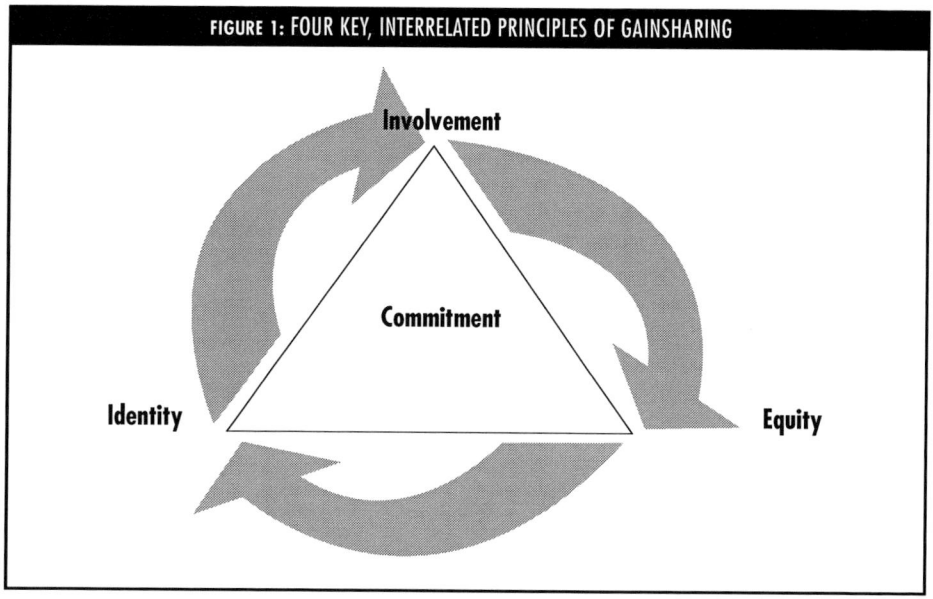

FIGURE 1: FOUR KEY, INTERRELATED PRINCIPLES OF GAINSHARING

have a strong desire to be respected for what they do. By sharing, the employer is communicating an important message to the work force, "We all contribute. That contribution is respected. Let's share the financial benefits."

Obviously, performance measures are established and a bonus calculation is developed to share the gains. Depending on the organization and its culture, a measurement system and subsequent methods of sharing are developed. Measures may be broad (e.g., ratio of cost to sales) or narrow (e.g., percent of scrap). Some companies have common-fate-oriented measures that are closely aligned with profit. Other companies have line-of-sight measures, of which employees feel they have more direct control. In some cases, there is only one measure, and in other cases, there are many measures. Regardless, when gains or losses are generated, and they are properly communicated, the result provides everyone in the organization with a common focus.

Gainsharing provides a method of keeping score. We all know how powerful a score can be for an athletic team when they are properly led, coached and developed. For example, in basketball, everyone in some way contributes to the final score. The starting five, the substitutes, the trainer, equipment manager and coach impact the result. In some cases, the impact may be negative. Regardless, everyone influences the outcome. The same is true for any organization. It just makes sense to share.

In my experience a bonus check is the best way to celebrate a win. Everyone seems to like money. One person may spend the bonus on himself/herself; others may use it for paying extra bills; and a more frugal person may save it. If the award is provided by some other means (e.g., deferred compensation, gift catalog points, extra days off), the common appeal is lessened.

The size of gainsharing bonuses typically ranges from 4 percent to 10 percent of compensation. However, it is not unprecedented to have bonuses exceed 20 percent. Generally, in the first year of a gainsharing plan, the payouts tend to be less than the norm, since people are just learning the new system and trying to develop a better understanding and awareness.

Sharing — and its impact on the sense of equity — is very powerful. The sense of fairness or equity runs very deep in human nature, regardless of race, creed, nationality or culture. The perception of equity can drive very strong emotions and promote feelings, such as the sense of fairness, trust and respect. Everyone wants to be treated equitably.

The principle of equity has a significant impact on the principle of identity. A business owner acts much differently than the workers. The owner has a very strong sense of identity to the operation. Many owners feel their business is part of them. When gains are shared, organizations begin to foster a similar feeling among their employees.

For example, if a factory shares 50 percent of the gain or loss in scrap, employees would in a sense own 50 percent of the value of the plant's scrap. The concept can direct a number of changes in one's actions and behaviors.

Identity

The principle of identity speaks to the sense of purpose, belonging, accountability and ownership. When performance is measured and communicated, and gains are financially shared, the work force develops an appreciation and understanding of the organization's needs and goals. The level of awareness is heightened as information is shared. Many questions are asked about the operation's performance, customer and overall business climate. Employees develop a better understanding and appreciation for the business. As understanding grows, the need for change is recognized. Change leads to improvement, and improvement leads to gains. Unfortunately, change is difficult, not only for the work force, but for members of management.

When performance problems occur, there is a stronger desire from the general work force to know more about the problem, causes and consequences. People question decisions. Problems that may have been overlooked in the past now have a direct financial impact on employees. In a sense, all of the organization's "warts" begin to surface. As managers are asked difficult questions, there is a need to explain, justify and perhaps admit mistakes. There is a tendency for people to hold one another more accountable. Identity can create more organizational stress. An increase in identity will have a major impact on the organization's culture. For gainsharing to be successful, the culture will need to evolve and change. A mentor of mine once stated that if a company implements a gainsharing plan, "management gives up its right not to listen." Otherwise the plan is destined to fail!

Building identity isn't easy. It takes time and effective communications, but as identity develops, employee and company goals become more common. Employees establish a sense of pride and ownership in the business. As identity grows, a common sense of belonging and teamwork develops. It fosters a "we" rather than an "us, them" attitude. Identity leads to involvement and participation.

Figure 2 on page 14 demonstrates how much employee identity improved, as determined by pre- and post-implementation surveys. The post-implementation survey was conducted one year after a Texas chemical plant implemented a gainsharing plan.

Involvement/Participation

Gainsharing cannot be successful without involvement. As identity and the sense of ownership are developed, employees naturally will have ideas on ways to improve performance. If there is no system to address ideas or if suggestions "fall on deaf ears," employees likely will become frustrated and give up. Gainsharing will become an incentive plan, a plan to work harder. And

FIGURE 2: COMPARISON OF PRE- AND POST-GAINSHARING SURVEY

SCALE

1	2	3	4	5
Strongly Disagree	Disagree	Neither Agree nor Disagree	Agree	Strongly Agree

Identity	Pre-Gainsharing	Post	% Change
1. My work contributes to the success of the company.	4.5	4.7	4%
2. Most employees here feel that their goals and the goals of the plant are pretty much the same.	3.5	3.8	8%
3. Employees here have a pretty good idea about how the economy will affect our business.	3.7	4.0	9%
4. The plant's overall goals and objectives are understood by employees.	3.5	3.9	10%

Note: Employee identity was relatively high before gainsharing; however, it even improved after the implementation of gainsharing.

we can only work so hard before we eventually risk burning out. On the other hand, involvement is a means of working smarter, and there are never-ending ways to do so. Involvement and working smarter foster continuous improvement.

Many managers have learned that the people performing the work often have solutions that best solve the problem. This rings true because workers are involved and more committed to implementing solutions. People support what they create. The solution may not be the same as one designed by an engineer. However, we all know that the best answer is the one that provides the best result.

If employees get more involved, it is important that managers recognize that they need to be willing to let people make a few mistakes along the way. Managers have to be brave enough to let go. Managers need to be willing to consult employees and openly listen to their opinions. The follow-up survey questions in Figure 3 on page 15 demonstrate management's willingness to do so. Survey results are based on the Texas chemical plant referred to earlier.

My favorite analogy takes me back to when my son was only about three or four years old. At the time, our home had about six acres of lawn. My son loved to ride on my lap as I mowed the lawn. When he was about five, I let him do some of the mowing. I stepped back and watched. He mowed. Of course the lawn wasn't done to perfection, but he was just learning. When he was finished, I would praise him and remark on a job well done. I would also offer a little encouragement and lawn mowing hints. You could see the pride in his face.

Today, my son has a very large landscaping company. He has a number of trucks and other large pieces of equipment. He has several crews of workers, but only one that mows lawns. Today my home has about 20 acres. Do you know who mows my lawn today? Not my son. His crew does the work. If I hadn't stepped back and let him become more involved, or if I was more critical than positive, who would be mowing my lawn today? By the way, when he was growing up I never paid him to mow, but we did have that "box" in the kitchen.

Unfortunately, employee involvement doesn't just happen. A system is needed to provide structure and discipline. Otherwise, there are no tools for

FIGURE 3: COMPARISON OF PRE- AND POST-GAINSHARING SURVEY

SCALE

1	2	3	4	5
Strongly Disagree	Disagree	Neither Agree nor Disagree	Agree	Strongly Agree

Participation	Pre-Gainsharing	Post	% Change
1. Management at this facility is interested in hearing employee's opinions on job related matters.	3.6	4.0	11%
2. Employees are generally consulted when decisions are made that affect them or their work.	2.7	3.1	15%

change. Generally, gainsharing plans include a team-based suggestion system as one of their main elements. The system gives people the opportunity to have their ideas heard, i.e., a system for listening. Everyone wants to be respected for what they do. A structured system to solicit, evaluate and implement employee ideas is a tool that can enhance respect throughout an organization.

When people receive feedback on their ideas and/or see their ideas implemented, they feel respected. When they receive a "thank you" or a pat on the back from a co-worker, manager or executive, they feel respected for their ideas and what they contribute. Hence, involvement leads to respect and respect breeds trust. In turn, trust results in a deeper level of respect.

Trust and respect further reinforce the principle of identity. As identity grows, so does the sense of ownership. When people have more ownership, they become more involved. As people become more involved, equity and financial rewards increase. Equity, identity and involvement are continually reinforced. However, without commitment, the most significant principle, the entire cycle can potentially collapse.

Commitment

Undoubtedly, the single most important principle for a gainsharing plan's success is the organization's commitment, particularly management's commitment to the process. Gainsharing doesn't run by itself. The managers' commitment drives involvement.

Managers need to be able to work together, support one another and set an example for the balance of the organization. They need to be competent in their respective roles and fields to lead, coach, train and help develop the work force. They need to be good listeners, respect their subordinates and recognize their contributions, and value the concept of more fully utilizing the company's human resources.

So, what does commitment mean?

First and foremost, managers must be committed as coaches and educators. They need to help employees gain a better understanding of the business and the role of employee involvement in gainsharing.

Managers need to have a strong feeling that it is "fair to share," and managers need to demonstrate support and commitment to the gainsharing plan.

Managers should:

- Hold regular departmental or organizationwide communications meetings
- Quickly report bonus results and discuss the "whys" behind the results
- Openly share conditions regarding the business
- Be committed to regular ongoing communications to further develop awareness and identity.

The involvement system is intended to push decision-making down. Some supervisors may view this as a loss of control and may not be willing to give up some of the decision-making. However, the objective is to provide an opportunity for employees to have more control of and influence over their work.

In addition, managers need to get involved. Some managers may feel that they do not need to formally submit ideas. However, managers need to lead by example and submit ideas. How can managers expect their employees to become more involved unless they participate, too? They need to "walk the talk."

Managers should be committed to providing the time, facility and/or resources for:

- Involvement team meetings
- Implementation of employee ideas and/or suggestions
- Ongoing training and employee development
- Recognition of employees who are actively involved.

Managers should help monitor team activity. They should visit involvement team meetings and serve as advisors and resource persons.

Finally, managers should monitor performance measures and occasionally make changes to ensure fairness for both the company and employees. I've seen some rather unique situations where the company improved in terms of profits and operational measures, but the bonus formula failed to generate a payout. Obviously, something was wrong. The formula needed to be changed.

A gainsharing plan must be managed. More management and employee commitment typically drives better performance, and better performance directs larger bonuses. Commitment drives equity.

The paramount importance of management commitment to and support for gainsharing is demonstrated in a follow-up survey conducted in two separate gainsharing facilities in Deer Park and Laporte, Texas. Both plants, part of the same corporation and located within six miles of each other, implemented the gainsharing plans at the same point in time. However, one year after implementation, there was a dramatic difference in how employees viewed their respective gainsharing plan. As Figure 4 demonstrates, the level of commitment from the Deer Park management team was a key difference.

FIGURE 4: COMPARISON OF PRE- AND POST-GAINSHARING SURVEY

SCALE

1	2	3	4	5
Strongly Disagree	Disagree	Neither Agree nor Disagree	Agree	Strongly Agree

Management Support	Pre-Gainsharing	Post	% Change
1. Management supports our gainsharing plan.	3.7	4.2	14%
2. Managers are doing all they can to help gainsharing succeed.	3.4	3.8	12%
3. Managers behave in a more participative manner since gainsharing was implemented.	3.3	3.7	12%
4. Management at this facility is interested in hearing employee opinions on job-related matters.	3.3	4.0	21%
5. My manager frequently asks for my ideas and suggestions.	3.3	3.9	18%
6. Plant management encourages open communications from employees.	3.3	4.1	24%
7. Top management encourages open communications from employees.	3.0	3.7	23%
Employee Satisfaction			
8. Employees are more satisfied now than before gainsharing.	3.1	3.9	26%
9. Since the plan began, employees have more control over their work life.	2.8	3.4	21%
10. This is a more enjoyable place to work now than it was before gainsharing.	2.9	3.7	28%

3

The Calculation Philosophy: Control or Common-Fate Orientation

I like to refer to a gainsharing plan's model, measures and bonus formula as the "calculation." After an understanding of the gainsharing philosophy has been developed, and organizational readiness has been thoroughly explored, organizations have to ask the question, "Why?" What is the primary purpose for installing a gainsharing plan? One might think that the answer obviously is to increase profits. Surprisingly, that is not always the case. I find in most cases, improved profit is one of many plan objectives. However, it is not typically the primary purpose. The primary purpose for a gainsharing plan is a function of the organizational culture and the business climate. A plan's purpose often is related to a desire to address some long-term organizational or cultural weakness.

Facilities fighting for survival may have a completely different purpose for gainsharing than a more fortunate facility that has seen only good times. Companies that have a successful employee involvement system install gainsharing to further support these efforts. Some organizations install plans because it reinforces their Six Sigma or Lean Manufacturing initiative. Facilities that have had a troubled past in terms of attitudes, trust and labor management problems may find that gainsharing's purpose lies more in terms of social and quality-of-work-life issues.

Figure 5 on page 23 provides a summary of gainsharing plan purpose statements written by design teams. These purpose statements share a common trait: they fail to reference sharing gains or a financial bonus as being the primary purpose. Employees typically agree that more money in their pockets is not the primary outcome of a successful gainsharing plan. The money is more of a result driven by many other goals.

Because organizations vary so widely, there is no one best formula that can be used as a cookie cutter for all organizations. Before developing a calculation, some critical issues need to be explored.

> **FIGURE 5: GAINSHARING PLAN PURPOSE STATEMENTS**
>
> The purpose of the plan is to promote employees working together throughout the organization toward a common set of goals.
>
> The purpose of the plan is to build respect between employees and the management team.
>
> The purpose of the plan is to improve trust in relationships at all levels.
>
> The purpose of the plan is to develop an environment in which all employees have one unified goal: teamwork.
>
> The purpose of the plan is to create an environment of continuous improvement in order to provide outstanding customer relations, strong financial performance, and greater associate commitment and satisfaction.
>
> The purpose of the plan is to improve performance through associate involvement.
>
> The purpose of the plan is to improve the long-term security of employees by continually improving performance.
>
> The purpose of the plan is to continually improve the plant operations in all key areas in order to be the most competitive plant in our industry.
>
> The purpose of the plan is for all associates to be aware that their actions impact our ability to reach our plant's specific goals.

Physical vs. Financial Measures

One way of looking at the type of calculation a company might use is to examine the dichotomy between physical and financial measures. Figure 6 makes this simple point. Let's say the Ajax Coal Company owns and operates a coalmine. A physical measure could be as simple as the number of tons of coal mined per hour worked.

For example, if workers historically mined 80 tons in 40 hours, their productivity (ratio of output to input) would be 2 tons per hour.

$$\frac{\text{Output}}{\text{Input}} = \frac{80 \text{ tons}}{40 \text{ hours}} = 2 \text{ tons per hour}$$

Let's say the president of Ajax tells employees that 50 percent of the productivity gains above the baseline of 2 tons per hour will be shared. After communicating the good news, the miners pull together and miraculously coal starts shooting up the conveyors at a record rate of 100 tons per 40-hour period. Physical productivity has now increased to 2.5 tons per hour.

$$\frac{\text{Output}}{\text{Input}} \quad \frac{100 \text{ tons}}{40 \text{ hours}} = 2.5 \text{ tons per hour}$$

In this case physical productivity increased by 25 percent. In turn, employees are paid a handsome bonus, 12.5 percent of the total financial gains from their increased productivity.

$$\frac{\text{Change in physical productivity}}{\text{Baseline}} \quad \frac{(2.5 - 2) = .5}{2 \text{ tons per hour}} = 25\%$$

I refer to a physical measure as control-oriented. If the miners work a little harder or smarter, there will be a gain. Better teamwork, cooperation and communications between shifts certainly will help generate a gain. The miners have a significant impact on their output. There will be a direct line of sight between their performance and pay. This linkage likely will result in improved productivity.

On the other hand, the Ajax Company may select a financial formula (e.g., sales per hour worked). Let's say that coal is selling for $20 per ton. During the base period, financial productivity is calculated to be $40 of sales per hour worked.

$$\frac{\text{Output}}{\text{Input}} \quad \frac{(\$20 \times 80 \text{ tons}) = \$1,600}{40 \text{ hours}} = \$40 \text{ of sales per hour}$$

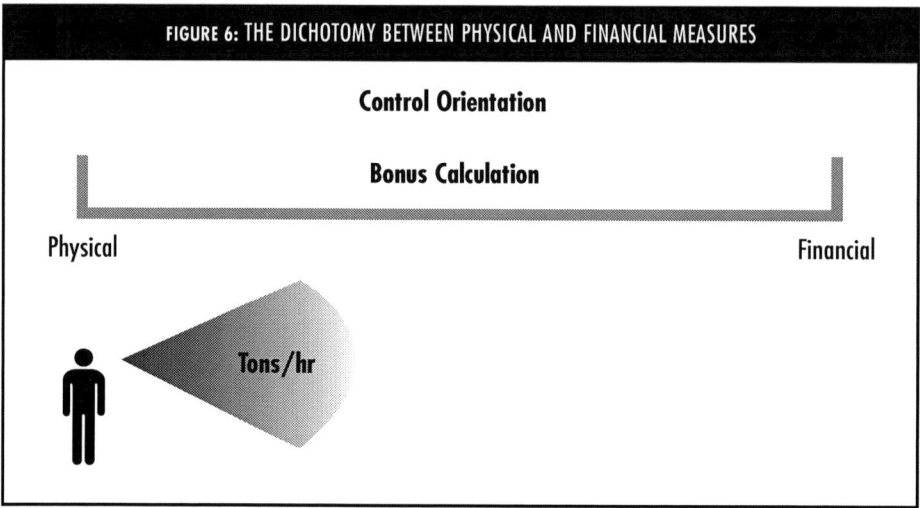

FIGURE 6: THE DICHOTOMY BETWEEN PHYSICAL AND FINANCIAL MEASURES

In turn, the company president proudly presents the new sales/hour formula to the miners. As with the previous example, 100 tons of coal is mined in only 40 hours. The miners focus on their jobs while thinking how they will spend their anticipated bonus. However, the president fails to inform them that the winter is much more mild than anticipated, and that solar energy is becoming a popular alternative to fossil fuels. Coal prices are depressed. The vice president of sales recognizes the importance of maintaining market share, and grudgingly reduces the selling price to $10 per ton. Financial productivity has now plunged to $25 of sales per hour worked.

$$\frac{\text{Output}}{\text{Input}} \quad \frac{(\$10 \times 100 \text{ tons}) = \$1,000}{40 \text{ hours}} = \$25 \text{ of sales per hour}$$

In turn, the president sadly announces that there is no bonus forthcoming since financial productivity declined by more than 37 percent.

$$\frac{\text{Change in financial productivity}}{\text{Baseline}} \quad \frac{\$25 - \$40 = -\$15}{\$40 \text{ per hour}} = -37.5\%$$

The physical measure provided a gain, and the financial measure did not. The world has remained the same, the miners are working just as hard, and the president is faced with the same market conditions.

I refer to a financial measure as "common fate." The company and employees will experience the same good and the same bad. As the company profits, the president, the workers and the bonus are linked together.

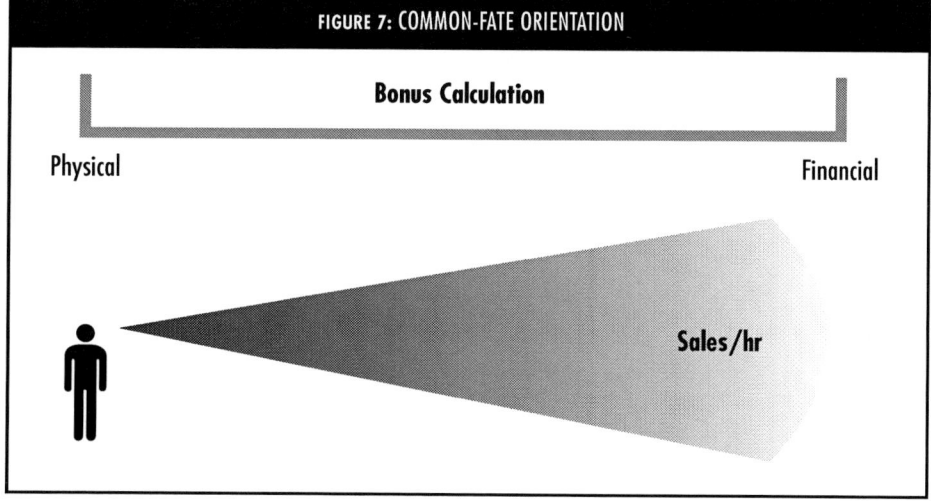

FIGURE 7: COMMON-FATE ORIENTATION

However, the line of sight between the miners' work and what they are paid has greatly diminished.

Workers would argue that they have no *control* over the selling price and market conditions. They have done everything they could to generate a gain. Obviously, the miners would prefer the physical measure of tons per hour.

On the other hand, the president may prefer the financial calculation, the argument being, "How much longer can I continue to pay out a bonus when the selling price is going down? If this continues I will be forced to board up the shaft and close the mine."

That is why it is so critical for organizations to examine and clearly define why they want to install a gainsharing plan. What is the purpose of the plan? Does the organization want to change behaviors by maximizing the line of sight between performance and pay, or does it want to reinforce the concept of "common-fate." An organization in a survival mode may take one approach, while a highly profitable one may take another.

In addition, an organization's ability to use a financial calculation (rather than a physical one) may be more limited because of cultural and human resources issues. How open is the company's communication? How knowledgeable are employees about the business conditions? What is the trust level? How much baggage is the organization carrying from its past? To address these and other questions, the organization needs to examine its employee involvement climate and culture.

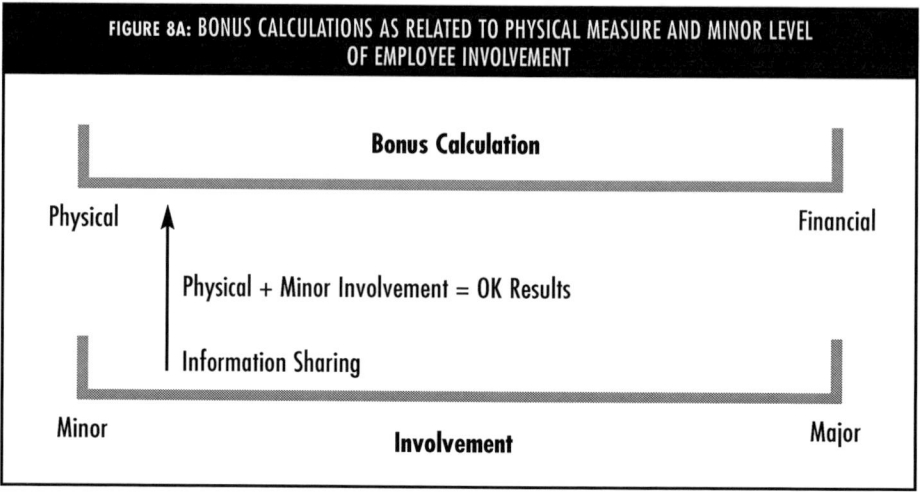

FIGURE 8A: BONUS CALCULATIONS AS RELATED TO PHYSICAL MEASURE AND MINOR LEVEL OF EMPLOYEE INVOLVEMENT

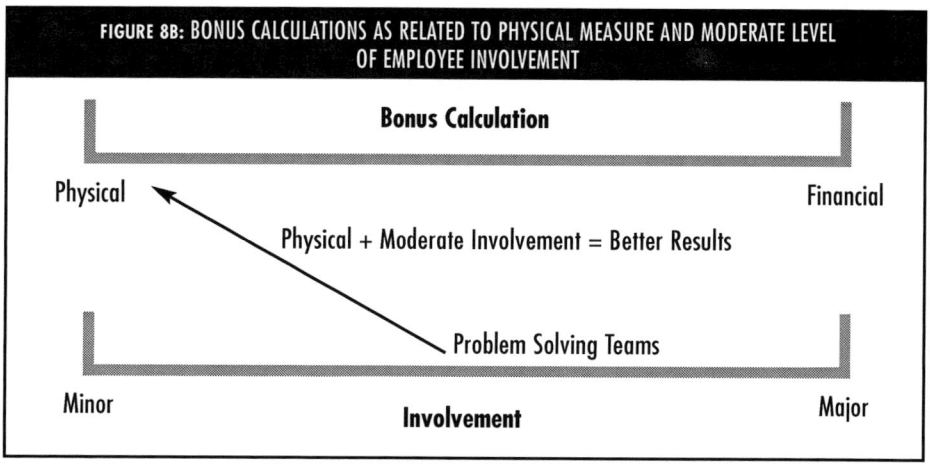

FIGURE 8B: BONUS CALCULATIONS AS RELATED TO PHYSICAL MEASURE AND MODERATE LEVEL OF EMPLOYEE INVOLVEMENT

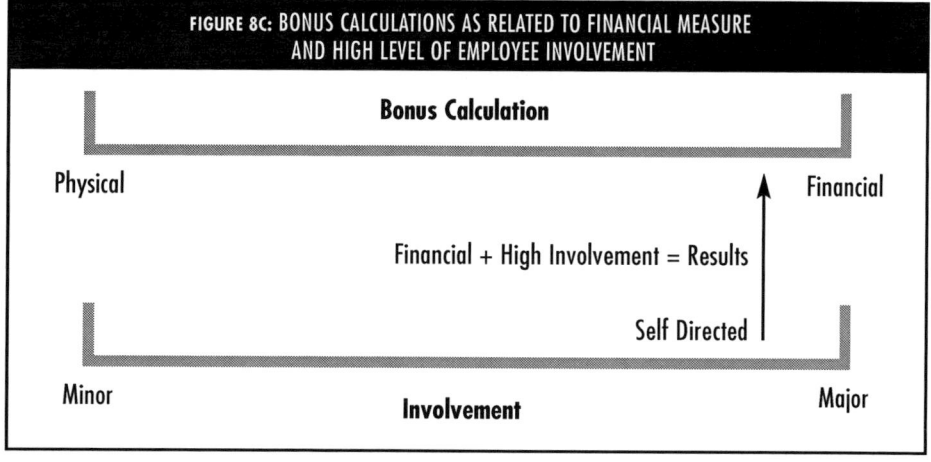

FIGURE 8C: BONUS CALCULATIONS AS RELATED TO FINANCIAL MEASURE AND HIGH LEVEL OF EMPLOYEE INVOLVEMENT

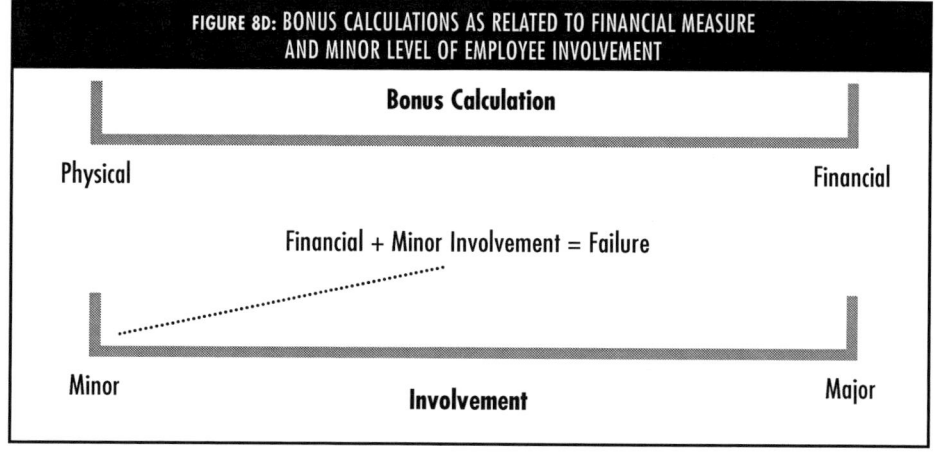

FIGURE 8D: BONUS CALCULATIONS AS RELATED TO FINANCIAL MEASURE AND MINOR LEVEL OF EMPLOYEE INVOLVEMENT

Employee Involvement — Minor vs. Major

Another dichotomy to consider when exploring the calculation relates to the level of employee involvement in the organization. The level of employee involvement can be anywhere from a minor degree (almost none) to a major degree. (See Figures 8A to 8D.) A minor degree of involvement could be regular communication and information sharing. For example, weekly postings of performance charts are a form of minor involvement. On the contrary, a major degree of involvement could be found in a factory environment where all employees participate in self-directed work teams.

Let's return to the coalmine example and how the Ajax president is proceeding with the gainsharing design. The company president elects to have a gainsharing plan and adopts a physical calculation. In addition, management style has been very traditional. People are closely supervised and directed. The level of involvement is quite low. There are no teams or problem-solving groups. However, the company president daily posts productivity figures, highlighting the month-to-date gain or loss. The coal miners see and easily understand the postings of tons per hour mined for the day. They compare actual performance to the baseline of 2 tons per day. Could we likely see productivity improve? Yes, there is a strong line of sight between performance and the bonus. The workers are receiving daily feedback, and awareness is heightened. (See Figure 8A.)

Let's say that the company advances to a higher degree of involvement by training and instituting group problem-solving teams. Perhaps one team is working on a conveyor system problem and another on a grinding bit issue. Would performance continue to improve? Yes. Even better, the miners are working a little smarter. (See Figure 8B.)

A neighboring coalmine, The Sussex Coal Company, is also implementing a gainsharing plan. The culture at Sussex, however, is much different than that of Ajax.

The level of employee involvement at Sussex is extremely high. All of the miners participate in self-directed work teams. Among many other things, the Sussex teams interview and select new hires, schedule work and participate in setting their own budget. The president invests considerably in training and employee development. Also, the supervisors' role at Sussex is much different than at Ajax. The Sussex supervisors have gone through extensive training and serve as trainers, coaches and coordinators of team activities.

In terms of the calculation, the Sussex president selects a financial calculation, return on assets. The bonus results are not only posted, but regular meetings are conducted to review results including profit, loss, expenses, new business opportunities, etc. In addition, the Sussex vice president of sales regularly meets with the coalminers regarding competitors' offerings, market share and the threats of solar energy. Sussex has a financial calculation supported by an extremely high level of employee involvement. Could the Sussex gainsharing plan work? Yes.

There is obviously a high level of commitment and involvement by everyone. The miners have a high degree of understanding and *identity* to the business. The organization is extremely open. The miners almost feel like owners. (See Figure 8C.)

Finally, let's turn back to Ajax. After observing the success of the Sussex gainsharing, the Ajax president decides to take a different approach with the Ajax gainsharing design. The president decides to utilize the Sussex financial calculation, rather than the physical, control-oriented measure of tons per hour worked. Also, the Ajax president greatly overestimates the true level of employee involvement found in his company's environment. There are no teams, no regular meetings on results. In fact, the supervisors have a very traditional and autocratic style. No one listens to the workers or their ideas and suggestions. However, there are some written communications at Ajax. Once a quarter, the company publishes an attractive quarterly statement reporting profitability and the bonus results. In fact, the statement is even sent to employee's homes.

What happens to the Ajax gainsharing plan? Do behaviors change? Does the culture advance? How are the four gainsharing principles of equity, identity, involvement and commitment impacted? Clearly the Ajax plan is a failure. Ajax is too aggressive in adopting a financial rather than a physical calculation. A financial calculation in an environment with low involvement is destined for failure. (See Figure 8D.) Companies that have successful gainsharing plans with a financial calculation must be extremely committed. Much communication, training and involvement needs to take place. Herein lies the reason many profit-sharing plans fail to motivate and engage the work force.

A small privately held company has a better chance of success with a financial calculation than a large multisite corporation. There are always exceptions, but the level of employee identity often is higher at smaller companies. There is more loyalty and allegiance between employee and owner. The line of sight between profits and what employees do is closer than that found in a large organization. In larger companies, employees are more likely to say, "The people at the top don't know me. They are only looking out for themselves. You can't trust them. How can I trust someone I can't see? How can I be expected to trust the financial numbers they report?" If this is the environment, a physical calculation is more appropriate.

In short, organizations with a relatively high level of involvement have more choice in the type of formula that can work: physical vs. financial. That is not to say that organizations with low involvement should avoid gainsharing. It also doesn't mean that organizations must first install a comprehensive involvement system before installing gainsharing. The principles of equity and involvement are reinforcing. However, a low involvement organization has to be very guarded in selecting the appropriate calculation.

Companies recognizing this fact initially may have a gainsharing plan with a physical, control-oriented calculation. With time, communications and training, the level of employee involvement is advanced. Some companies continue long-term with a physical or operational calculation. Others evolve from a physical to a more financial and common-fate calculation. Donnelly Mirrors and Herman Miller are two such examples.

After thoroughly defining the purpose of an organization's gainsharing plan and where the organization stands in terms of employee involvement, there is one more critical element. "What happens if there are no profits? Will the organization still be willing to pay out a gainsharing bonus?" These questions need to be fully explored before developing a calculation.

Operating Performance vs. Profits

The big question is, "What do we do when operating performance improves, and profits go down?" (See Figure 9 and corresponding scenarios.) Many companies use gainsharing as a tool to promote and drive operational measures

FIGURE 9: OPERATING PERFORMANCE & PROFITS MATRIX

		Company Profits Up	Company Profits Down
Operating Performance	Up	A	C
	Down	D	B

such as productivity, raw material usage, scrap, returns, on-time deliveries, customer service, machine uptime, cost per unit and countless other measures that enhance the organization's effectiveness.

Scenario A shows that operating performance *and* company's profits have improved. If you owned the company, would you pay a bonus? Most would say, "yes." We can discuss how later. Scenario A is pretty easy. A few may say, "no." In that case, there is no support for the principle of equity, and it makes no sense to move forward in exploring gainsharing.

Scenario B is another easy one. Both operating performance and profits are down. In this scenario, no one would pay out a bonus unless they just wanted to give money away. Surprisingly, in the old days some companies actually did this in terms of a year-end discretionary bonus. Basically, the bonus was an entitlement. Employees didn't understand why they got it, but they liked it. However, in years in which the bonus was smaller or there was no bonus at all, employees complained that the company was cheating them.

Scenario C. Now the decision-making is a little tougher. Let's say operating performance is outstanding: productivity at record levels, no product returns, customer satisfaction at an all time high, zero scrap, etc. However, profits are down. Would you pay a bonus? Some will say, "yes," and others, "no." Some may say, "It depends on why profits were down." Perhaps profits are down due to pricing issues and the recent acquisition of another company. Maybe the company has a major loss for the second consecutive quarter.

Those who argue, "yes" for paying a bonus clearly support the physical, control-oriented concept. They will say, "Employees did all they were asked." They will argue for line of sight. "Employees have no direct control over profits." They will argue that the improvements in operating performance are long-term, that the company will reap the benefits for years. They will debate, "If there were no improvements in the operating measures, profits would have been much worse." Some might even argue, "Don't worry about it. Scenario C can't happen, because the operational measures we've selected directly tie to profits."

Others will argue that a bonus should not be paid. The "no" people support the financial, common-fate philosophy. "After all, where is the money for a bonus coming from? We will be pushed into further debt. There's no way."

Some may debate, "It depends. Maybe there should be a payout, but not as much." There are ways to design such a plan. A company that has a plan with operational or physical measures may include a profitability gate or multiplier. However, employees, particularly in a culture with low involvement, may not trust a profit gate.

What's the right answer? Yes, no, maybe? It gets back to the purpose for installing the plan. It depends on the organizational culture. If the culture is one in which employees are informed, trust levels are positive and the employees are highly engaged, the answer may be, "no bonus if there are low profits." On the other hand, if the answers to these issues are less positive, the answer may be "yes, even if profits are low."

Scenario D. Operating performance down, profits up, would you pay out? "No" appears to be the logical choice, unless you want to have a traditional profit-sharing plan. The physical, control-oriented advocates may argue that the financial, common-fate advocates want to have it both ways. The control-oriented advocates may argue that, "When employees perform, and profits are down, you won't pay. When profits are up and performance down, you won't pay. You financial people want to have your cake and eat it, too."

On the other hand, the common-fate advocates may debate, "We are only willing to pay if the organization wins by achieving its profit targets, and we will be happy to share if employees perform." I'm familiar with at least one organization that uses this philosophy. They refer to their plan as "Win Share."

Regardless of one's thinking on these issues, the management team needs to have a thorough discussion before moving forward with gainsharing. I cannot emphasize this issue enough. If not, there may be surprises down the road, which will result in major human resources and trust issues. However, once this decision is made, the next important question is, "What is the group that will share in the gains?"

4

The Distribution Group: Boundaries

Generally, gainsharing is site-specific and includes everyone at the site. A few exceptions exist, such as when a manufacturing site houses a regional sales manager or customer service group. These people often serve a number of sites and only provide minor support to the site in question. At times these employees are not included in the plan, or they receive a partial share. However, a critical initial decision needs to be addressed: What is the group that will share in the gains; what are the boundaries for participation? This decision defines the distribution group or groups for measuring and sharing gains.

The distribution group refers to departments, business units and other organizational units at the site. Performance may be measured separately for each group. The question is: Should the gain from all the groups be pooled and, in turn, shared with all the eligible participants? Perhaps the gains for each group should be measured separately and distributed independently. In this case, one group may receive a bonus for the period, and another may not. These and other related questions will have a major impact on the site's culture and how people interact. The sense of fairness and equity will be greatly influenced. The consequences of these decisions will have a significant impact on the business and human resources climate.

The more a group can directly be paid for its gain, the greater the line of sight. On the contrary, the line of site for a worker on piecework is extremely narrow. (See Figure 10 on page 37.) Many factory managers and compensation professionals know that the exchange theory of compensation has an adverse impact in environments with individual incentive plans.

On the other hand, if all measures are socialized, there may be no changes in behavior. People may say, "We can't gain because the other group is always pulling performance down." A socialized system may not promote accountability.

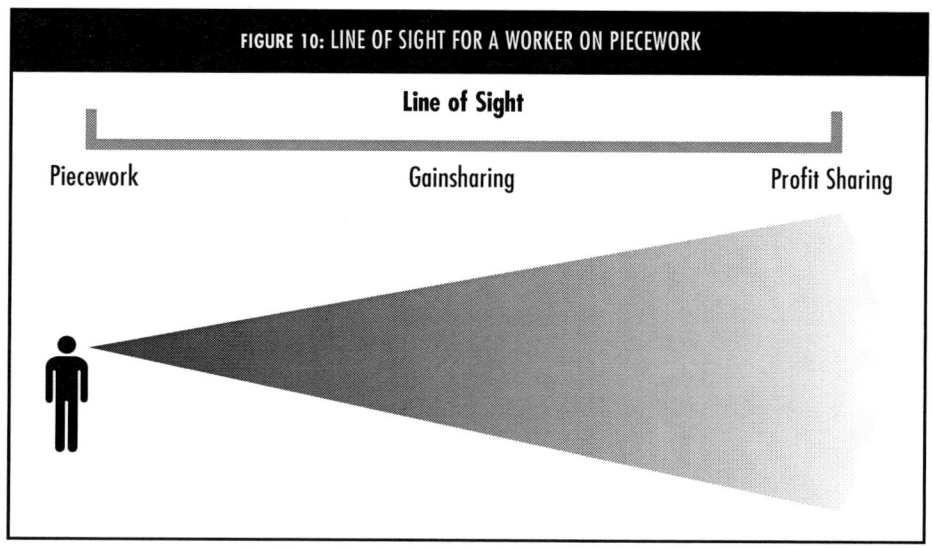

FIGURE 10: LINE OF SIGHT FOR A WORKER ON PIECEWORK

Gainsharing Implementation Case Study

I recently was involved in supporting a gainsharing implementation for a major automotive supplier in St Louis. The union facility employs approximately 270 people. More than half of the employees worked on individual piecework. Management and union officials jointly explored gainsharing and agreed to move forward with a plan. The first step was to eliminate the piecework system since the behaviors driven by piecework run counter to the gainsharing's teamwork philosophy. Both management and union agreed that piecework was a management tool from the past, and change was necessary for the long-term security and viability of the business. A design team consisting of 16 employees represented a cross section of the work force, including two top managers. The first step was for team members to develop the purpose statement and the plan's supporting goals. In short, why did they want to install a plan? What outcomes did the team want to achieve? After much discussion, the following purpose statement was developed: *To improve job security, create a more viable operation and promote more business.* In other words, the design team viewed gainsharing as a tool for survival.

The distribution group(s) for the automotive supplier plant happened to be relatively simple. However, it will be helpful to review some of the plant's basic alternatives.

Figure 11 provides four general methods of measuring and distributing gains.

FIGURE 11: DISTRIBUTION ALTERNATIVES

	Measures	Distribution Group
1	Broad Measures	Common Group
2	Narrow Measures	Common Group
3	Narrow Measures	Independent Groups
4	Narrow Measures	Blended Groups

Broad Measurement — Common Distribution Group

The automotive supplier plant has three manufacturing departments: Foundry, Original Equipment (OE) and After Market. In addition, the plant has typical support groups, such as tooling, maintenance, shipping, quality and office support. Cost per unit is an example of a broad measure for a typical manufacturing facility. The productivity ratio is as follows:

$$\frac{\text{Input}}{\text{Output}} = \frac{\text{Total plant cost}}{\text{Total good units produced}}$$

In this model, total plant good units are the output, regardless of the department in which they are produced (Foundry, Original Equipment or After Market). The input, total manufacturing cost, again is measured plantwide. The measure is fairly broad. Obviously, if costs are reduced and units stay the same, or if costs stay the same and units increase, there will be a gain.

As demonstrated in Model 1 (Figure 12 on page 39), the gains are shared with all employees from one common pool, regardless of their department. Model 1 reinforces the idea that everyone in the plant needs to focus on the common goal of reducing the manufacturing cost per unit or increasing units. Employees, regardless of their position, in some way impact the ratio. If the receptionist isn't helpful to a customer, the plant might lose a potential account. There is no question that better cooperation and collaboration will help generate gains. Figure 12 reinforces the

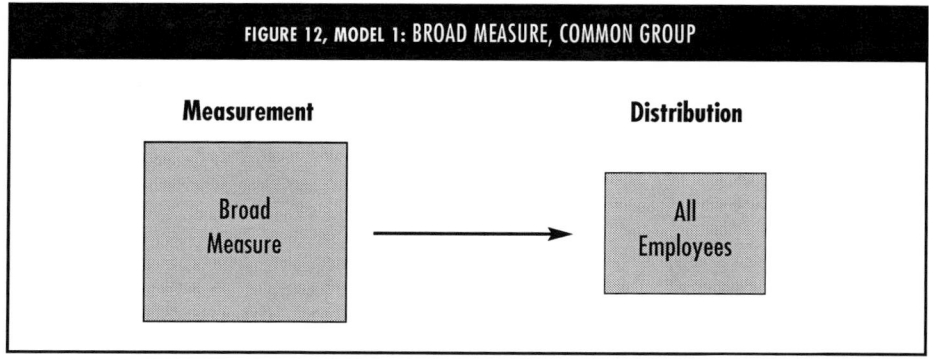

concept that there is one *team* at the St. Louis site. The model certainly supports the plan's purpose: job security and viability of the operations.

On the down side, the broad measure of total cost per unit limits the line of sight. For example, the OE employees don't clearly see their department's contribution to the gain. In addition, employees may have difficulty seeing how their efforts impact expenses such as depreciation, insurance, taxes, etc. The measure is broad. It falls somewhere in the middle of the physical/financial continuum. In light of the former piecework culture, the line of sight may be too far to significantly influence behaviors. (See Figure 13.) The design team agreed that Model 1 was not a fit for operations.

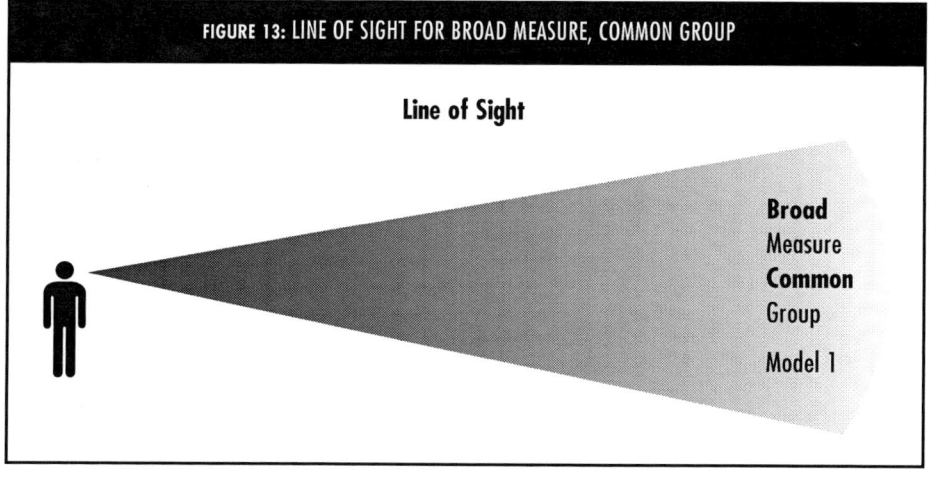

Narrow Measures, Common Group

Another approach is to measure productivity separately for the three manufacturing units. (See Figure 14, Model 2.)

Rather than measuring productivity in a broad sense (cost per unit), the productivity measure is narrower (units per hour worked).

$$\frac{Output}{Input} = \frac{Good\ units}{Hours\ worked}$$

Tooling cost, a second measure, is a significant part of the operations and can be directly impacted by employee efforts. Therefore, tooling cost per unit of output is added as a second measure to the model. To increase the line of sight, the manufacturing department measures tooling cost. Obviously, quality is extremely important, so scrap is a third measure. Scrap, tooling cost and units per hour are all elements of the broader total cost per unit in Model 1. As done previously, gains are pooled and shared commonly with all participants. The "one-team concept" is still reinforced.

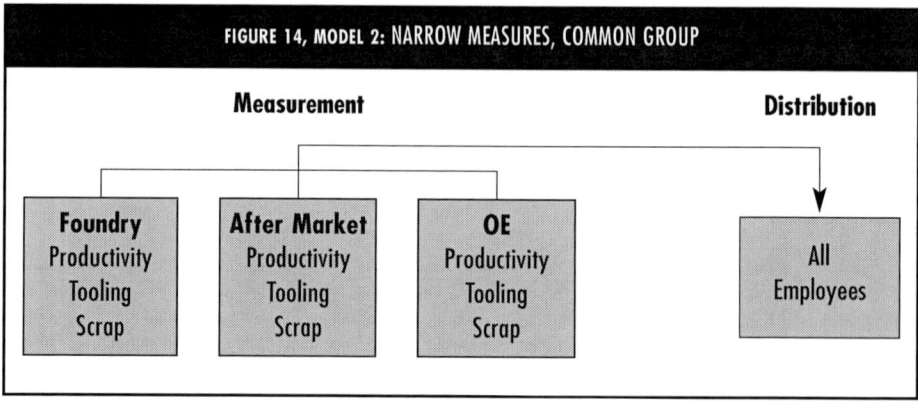

The line of sight in Model 2 is definitely sharper than Model 1. (See Figure 15 on page 41.) Employees from each department can easily see their contribution to the common pool. I worked with a privately held extrusion company that has a model similar to Model 2. Weekly results are posted on the Monday of the proceeding week. Employees often gather at the scoreboard as the results are posted to see their efforts. Department gains are in green and losses in red. Obviously no one wants to be in the red. There is a high degree

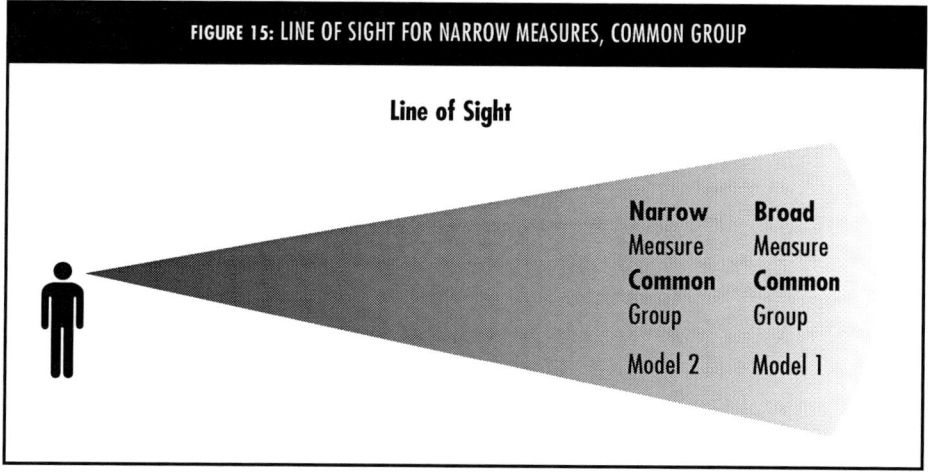

FIGURE 15: LINE OF SIGHT FOR NARROW MEASURES, COMMON GROUP

of awareness and identity to the results. Even though there is a greater line of sight, there is the potential of complaints and finger pointing. Therefore, the situation must be properly managed. In addition, if measures are too narrow, there is a potential for suboptimization by employees not focusing on perhaps other critical operating variables.

As a plant manager once told me, "Be careful what you measure (what you want to improve), because you can very possibly get it."

Narrow Measures, Independent Group

In Model 3 (Figure 16), the same measures are being employed as in Model 2. However, the gains are shared independently for the three manufacturing departments (Foundry, OE, and After Market). The support departments share in a common pool. Gains and losses from the three manufacturing departments are shared on a proportional basis with the support groups. The linkage is even greater in Model 3 than Model 2. Each manufacturing department would stand independently. This is particularly true for the three manufacturing departments. If Model 3 were used, there should be no, or very limited, independence between Foundry, OE, and After Market.

However, Model 3 still reinforces the need for the support groups to cooperate with and assist the manufacturing departments. If support groups strictly focused on helping the OE department at the expense of After Market and Foundry, the common pool would be adversely impacted.

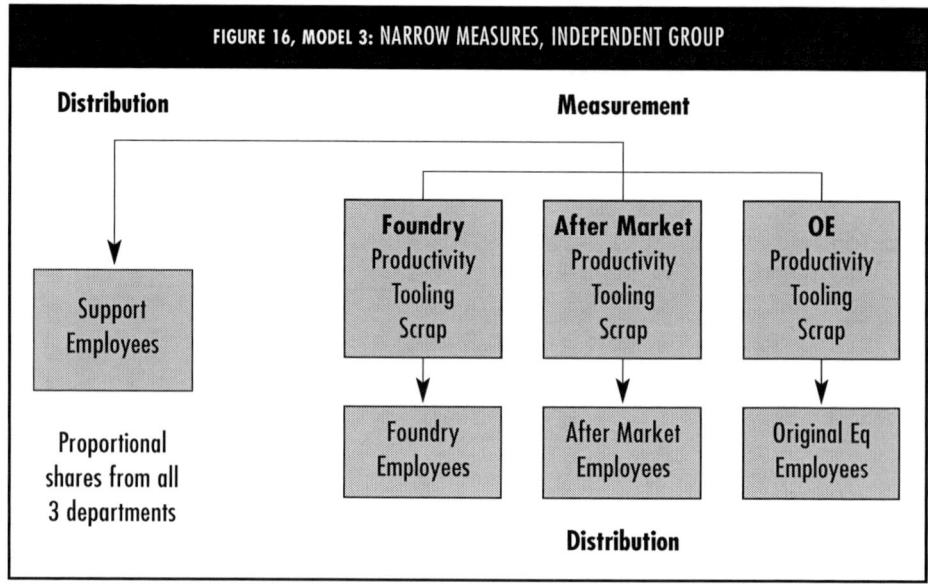

A key question that must be addressed in Model 3 is: How interdependent are the Foundry, After Market and Original Equipment departments?

If the line of sight becomes too close, however, there will be a lack of cooperation between departments. (See Figure 17.) The result could be very disconcerting to operations. Clearly, employees in one manufacturing department have little incentive to help the other. What is the likely outcome if the OE group fails to earn a bonus for several months and the After Market group

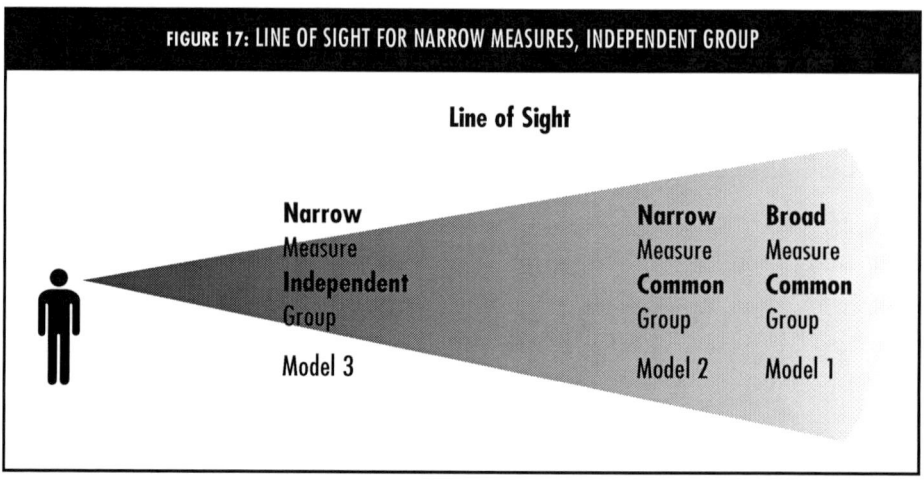

is performing at exceptional levels? What happens if the economy goes into recession? Sales and production volume in the OE business will decline as people buy fewer automobiles. On the other hand, business volume in After Market will increase as the public repairs older vehicles. The odds are that employees in After Market will have a better opportunity for gains than employees in OE. Will the OE employees become demoralized? What will happen in the lunchroom when the After Market people show off their gainsharing checks to their OE friends? Will OE employees feel that they are being treated unfairly? Will the OE group accuse management of providing proportionally more support, resources and equipment to the After Market group? Will OE remind management that After Market just installed a new furnace; "Why can't OE get a new one?"

The closer the line of sight, the greater the potential risk to the organization as a whole. There needs to be a balance.

Narrow Measures, Blended Group

A middle ground, between Model 2 and 3, is shown in Model 4, Figure 18. The gains again are measured separately. However, a portion of the gain from one group is shared with the other. That also would mean that a loss

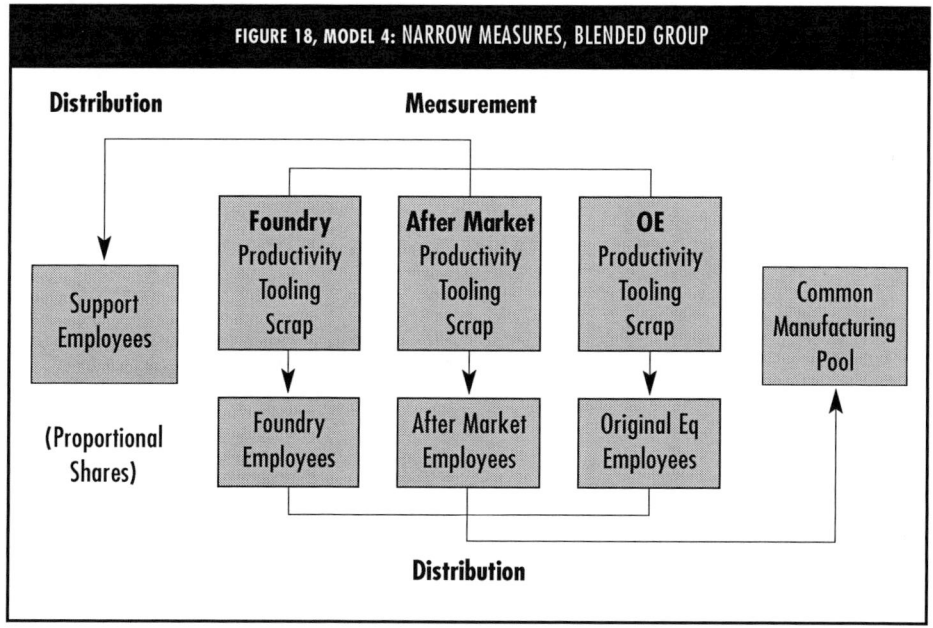

FIGURE 18, MODEL 4: NARROW MEASURES, BLENDED GROUP

in OE would take away from some of the gains distributed to employees in the Foundry and After Market departments. In terms of the support department's distribution, the gain they receive would remain the same as in Models 2 and 3.

In Model 4, the line of sight for employees in the manufacturing departments is somewhat more clouded than Model 3, but clearer than Model 2. (See Figure 19.) Model 4 might make sense if there is some interdependence between the manufacturing departments, but it is limited. The more the interdependence, the greater the portion of the department's gain flows to the common manufacturing pool. In Model 4, each group feels some of the others' gain and loss.

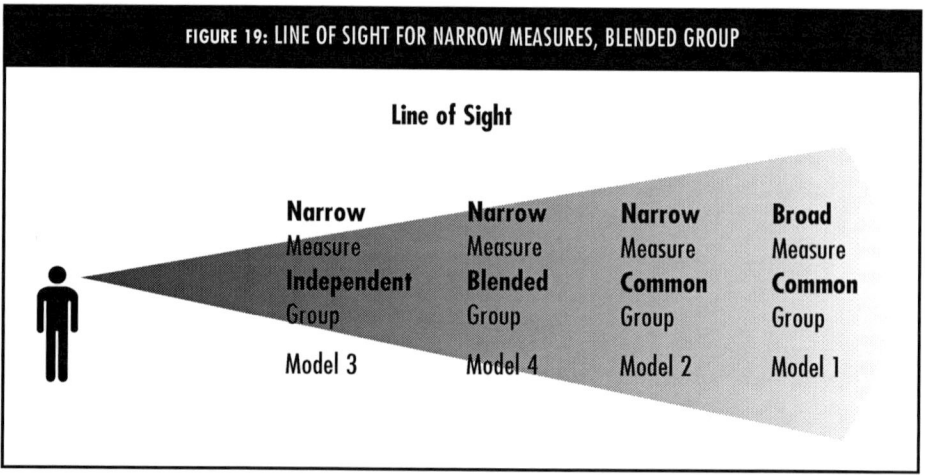

FIGURE 19: LINE OF SIGHT FOR NARROW MEASURES, BLENDED GROUP

The blended approach is certainly more complicated. However, I've seen it work very effectively. A plastics plant has a successful plan with a distribution approach similar to Model 4. The site has two business units in different buildings on the same grounds. Historically there was no need for collaboration between the two manufacturing units. Employees rarely transferred across department boundaries. Before gainsharing, employees had stronger identity to their business unit/department than to the company as a whole.

On the other hand, I've seen at least one case where the blended approach failed, and the company modified the plan to the common distribution group described in Model 2. In this case, an ink manufacturing company had a gainsharing plan for several years with one broad measure and a common distribution group similar to Model 1. As the company grew, more branch sites were added across the Midwest, while the line of sight diminished. Consequently, the plan was modified to provide a more narrow measure and blended distribution groups. Therefore, the payouts varied by site. After the first year the company average bonus was 3.5 percent of wages with one location receiving a 9 percent bonus and two receiving no bonus. Locations that received no bonus bitterly complained that they were not treated fairly in relationship to the higher bonus branches. Even though the measures were narrower, these employees felt a number of things outside of their control had an adverse effect on bonus results. After about two years, the company again modified the plan to a "narrow measure — common group" approach as described in Model 2. I'm not necessarily saying that this was the right decision. However, in the ink company, employees had a much stronger identity to the company as a whole. The culture was one in which employees historically had a great deal of pride in the company, regardless of where they worked. This was unlike employees' identity in the plastics plant, where allegiance was to their department and business unit. What is successful in one organization may not fit the culture of another.

I also should point out that a number of blended distribution models could be designed. As an alternative to Model 4, you can have one broad, organizationwide measure that is shared with all groups and more narrow group measures that are shared only within the group. Again, it depends on the gainsharing plan's purpose. Nevertheless, the following considerations should help determine the distribution of gains and boundaries.

Factors to Consider — Defining the Group

Interdependence — In most operations, considerable collaboration and cooperation between departments and work groups are essential. For example, in a tire manufacturing operation, the process flows from receiving, compounding, mixing, extruding, assembly, curing, finishing and shipping. In addition, the lab, maintenance and office groups are actively involved in supporting the process. In this case, one common distribution group would make sense. If this operation developed a model for department measures and multiple distribution groups, "silos would sprout up." The result could be devastating. Conversely, a large chemical plant may host several business units with each business unit's process having little dependence and interaction with the other. The plant may have a common maintenance and administrative support group. In such a case, a blended or hybrid distribution model may be more appropriate.

Administration — The greater the number of distribution groups, the more complex the design. More administrative time would be required to develop the plan. As employees transfer from one group to another, complex procedures to properly allocate bonus payouts would burden the organization. Employees would have difficulty understanding the model, so this would require follow-up training and communications.

Influence — Most companies that install gainsharing plans desire to maximize the pay-for-performance concept. On the other hand, if the line of sight is too close, the result may lead to suboptimization and a lack of teamwork and cooperation. People would focus on their group's immediate measures rather than the big picture. The plan could be saddled with many of the same problems created by piecework incentive plans. The result could potentially be devastating to the culture and performance of the operations. Remember, gainsharing is very much a team concept.

Identity — There is no doubt that gainsharing builds identity. Some companies have had gainsharing in place for a long time. We have all seen companies change their business strategy by changing a factory operation from a "cost center" to a "profit center." Subsequently, the operations may be decentralized and restructured into two or three business units. In these cases, I've seen companies change the distribution model from one common distribution group to a more complex blended/hybrid model. Clearly, the gainsharing plan must support the business strategy. Where does the organization want to drive identity: to the total organization, facility, business unit or department?

Inequities — The more the distribution groups, the greater are the perceptions of employee inequities. Gainsharing is not a perfect system. No matter what is measured, it is impossible for employees and the organization to have 100 percent control of performance. Many outside business factors may influence the gain. One group might have several successful months because of sheer luck. Another group might be doing a great job on things that it controls. However, no gain may be generated because of outside variables. Perhaps half the work force may become demoralized. This will impact the sense of equity. Emotions stemming from the perceptions of equity or fairness run very deep. When people complain about their pay, it is not so much in terms of the amount of pay. The emotional issue is how *they* are paid in relationship to someone else.

In the case of the St. Louis automotive supplier operations, it decided on Model 2, narrow measures — common group. Given the purpose of its plan and the culture of the plant, this clearly was the best alternative.

Typically, after considering these five issues (interdependences, influence, administration, identity and inequities), most organizations design plans that have a common distribution group. In most organizations, teamwork and collaboration between work groups and departments are critical. People working better together with one common focus can generate some of the largest gains.

5

Measurement

After the plan's purpose and goals have been developed and the boundaries for gainsharing have been defined, the next critical element in the plan development is determining what is to be measured. What does the organization want to drive? The measures help provide the common focus which in turn drives the "score."

There are as many potential combinations of measures as there are organizations. Historically, a single input/output ratio was used for gainsharing plans. A common approach was to measure gains based on the ratio of payroll cost to sales value of production. The Rucker Plan measured payroll cost in relationship to value added. IMPROSHARE used a physical measure of productivity, earned hours versus actual hours. In the 1980s, a multicost type formula grew in popularity (sales in relationship to selected expenses). (See Figure 20 on page 51 for an example of a multicost formula.)

The multicost model is relatively simple to develop and easy to understand. In the example, the ratio of value of production to a ratio of the sales to selected cost is 60 percent (the baseline). If the actual costs for the period are less than the expected, a gain will be generated. The multicost formula is relatively flexible. The organization can have a range of as many or few cost elements included in the base ratio. Typically, the fewer the cost elements, the greater the employee control and line of sight. In this example, material, depreciation and many other costs are excluded. Also, an organization may have multiple ratios, one for each product line or business unit.

However, today many organizations use multiple measures rather than the multicost approach. The multimeasure system is commonly referred to as a "family of measures" approach. (See Figure 21 on page 52.) Most organizations prefer customized arrangements of this type.

Basically, the family of measures approach uses three to six drivers of performance. The drivers are measured, and gains and losses calculated for each

FIGURE 20: MULTICOST SINGLE RATIO

Net Sales			$5,000,000
Inventory Change		+	$50,000
Sales Value of Production			$5,050,000
Baseline Ratio (cost/value of production)		x	60%
Expected Selected Cost			$3,030,000
Actual Selected Cost			
Wages and Salaries	$2,020,000		
Utilities	$353,500		
Factory Supplies	$252,500		
Office expenses	+ $50,500		
Total Selected Cost		−	$2,676,500
Gain			$353,500

Sharing

Employee Share %		x	30%
Employee Share			$106,050
Less Reserve for Deficit Months	50%	−	$53,025
Monthly Distribution			$53,025
Participating Payroll			$1,900,000
Bonus Percent	($53,025/$1,900,000)		2.8%

respective measure. The gains and losses are shared for each measure and then aggregated into an employee distribution pool. The pool is distributed to all participants. Generally, the measures are interrelated, so it is extremely important to aggregate the gains with the losses. For example, if productivity and quality were treated independently, there might be the tendency to focus only on one metric at the expense of the others. There needs to be a consequence for both good and bad performance. Some companies may initially begin gainsharing using only two or three measures. As the organization gains confidence in the system, it adds measures to the plan. However, companies often shy away from more than six measures for fear of a loss of employee focus.

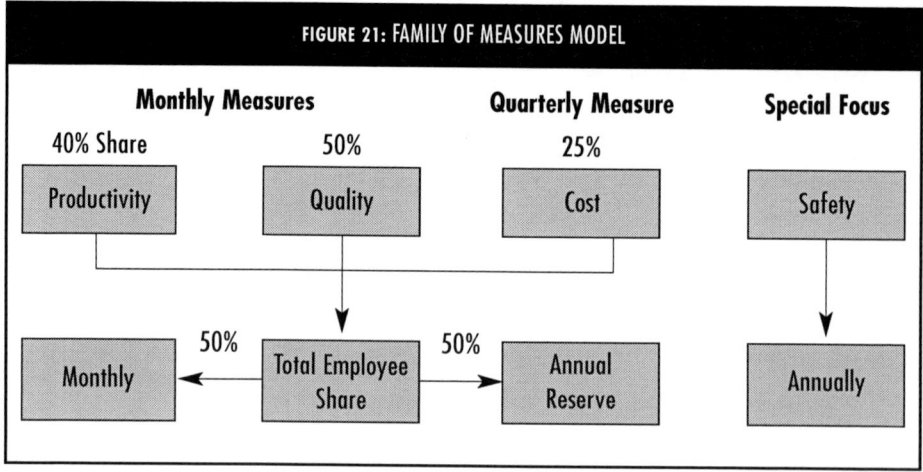

FIGURE 21: FAMILY OF MEASURES MODEL

Also, the employee share of the gain or loss from each measure may be different depending on employee controllability of the measure and its relative importance to the organization. Some organizations may change the employee sharing percentage for a particular measure from plan year to plan year, depending on economic conditions. For example, if a recession is anticipated, a company may decrease the sharing percent of the productivity measure and increase the sharing for the cost measure. The result will be better employee realignment with the organization's objectives.

A common approach is to divide the measures into two types: primary measures and special focus measures.

Primary measures calculate a direct financial gain and are self-funded. Scrap is an example of a primary measure. The following example calculates a true financial savings and gain to the organization.

```
Quality

Scrap
  Gross lbs.                8,500,000
  Baseline            x        2.00%
  Expected Scrap                            170,000
  Actual Scrap                          -   100,000
  Improvement in lbs.                        70,000
  Value/lbs.                         x        $0.25
Gain                                       $17,500
```

"Special focus" measures do not necessarily generate a true and direct financial gain, but are extremely important to the organization. Examples of special focus pools include OSHA recordables, on-time shipments, inventory accuracy and customer complaints. Since it is more difficult to calculate the financial gain for special focus pools, companies should budget for a potential payout from these measures. Figure 22 is an example of a special focus pool for safety. In the example, safety is paid annually and independently from all other measures. The objective of the measure is to reward for "strings" of accident-free months. For the first month of a string of zero accidents, $6 per employee will be awarded to a safety pool. For the second consecutive month of zero accidents, $12 per employee would be placed in the pool. For the third consecutive month, $18 will be added to the pool, and an additional $6 per employee will be added to the pool for each consecutive month. In a month that there is an accident, there will be $0 per employee added to the year-end pool. The award sequence will begin anew the following month at $6. In Figure 22, the accumulated sum of $166 per employee will be distributed based on the gainsharing plan's payment policies.

FIGURE 22: POOL ACCUMULATION

	Jan	Feb	Mar	Apr	May	Jun	Jul	Aug	Sep	Oct	Nov	Dec	Total
Number of Recordable accidents	0	0	0	0	0	0	1	0	0	0	1	0	
Contribution to Annual Pool	$6	$12	$18	$24	$30	$36	0	$6	$12	$18	0	$6	
Pool Accumulation	$6	$18	$36	$60	$90	$126	$126	$132	$142	$160	$160	$166	$166

Many organizations that include safety as a plan measure have a concern that the award system may cause employees not to properly report accidents. If this is the case, the following plan provision is commonly adopted:

> **Accuracy of reporting accidents:** In the event that an accident is not properly reported in order to generate a gain, the plant manager will call the design team to discuss its impact. If appropriate, the plant manager may suspend or terminate the plan.

Some companies elect not to use special focus pools, since they are not necessarily "self-funded." However, if both primary and special focus measures are used, I typically encourage more emphasis on the primary measures, since the gains are "green" (self-funded). Large payouts for "green dollar savings" are easier to explain to top management. I've seen some local managers get carried away with setting overly generous special focus pools ($2,400 per employee per year). Then, when the economy took a downward spiral, the local management had difficulty explaining to corporate why an average bonus of $2,400 per employee was justified, even though the facility had had an outstanding year in safety and on-time delivery performance. In other words, it is much easier to explain a $2,400 per employee annual payout when cost per unit has gone down by 5 percent, saving the company $350,000.

Primary measures are generally grouped into broad improvement categories. Companies might categorize measures in terms of productivity, quality, service, cost, energy, etc. The categories are not necessarily exclusive. One could make a good argument that cost and productivity are one in the same. The main objective is to make sure the organization has considered all the potential measures. Occasionally, when initially designing a plan, an organization can get off track by attempting to measure and reward activities rather than results. For example, companies may want to reward dollars to a special focus pool for 100 percent attendance of a safety meeting, or $20 to a pool for every suggestion submitted for the month. Generally, I have trouble with this concept. Instead, I encourage organizations to measure and reward results, not activities. The activities typically should not be rewarded; the activities are tasks that people perform that drive the result (measures). In turn, the measures generate the gains. Paying for activities not only is unfair to the owners or shareholders, it also hints of the exchange theory of compensation.

Advantages of the Family of Measures Approach

The family of measures approach has many advantages over the traditional single ratio approach. First and foremost, family of measures offers considerably more flexibility than the broader single ratio approach. Organizations can choose very specific drivers for success. The family of measures can be aligned with other organizational improvement initiatives. For example, I have worked with a company that has a major Six Sigma project focusing on improved cycle time. Therefore, cycle time is used as the measure for productivity.

Flexibility also is supported in that the sharing of one measure may be greater than another, thereby weighting the importance of each metric. As one employee stated, "The company is putting its money where its mouth is." Also, sharing percentages may change from one year to the next based upon changing business conditions. Some companies who have been in gainsharing for a number of years share a greater percent of a gain when a metric has achieved world-class performance levels. Also, a company may decide to increase the sharing of a measure if improvement opportunities are diminishing.

In some cases, the frequency of payout may vary by measure. For example, a company may share gains from productivity monthly, cost quarterly and safety annually. With multiple measures, the sharing frequency may vary. The family of measures approach also offers flexibility — a key advantage — in that measures may be added or changed over the years.

In addition to the flexibility advantages, family of measures provides very specific focus. Generally, workers can identify how they directly impact the measures. The result is an improved understanding and a better line of sight. Finally, since the family of measures approach generally utilizes narrower measures, the influence of external factors impacting the gain can be minimized.

However, these advantages are not without a cost. Plan development, design and implementation typically are more time-consuming than if a single ratio formula were used. Considerable time will be required to sort through all the possible measures and evaluate the pros and cons. More modeling will be required to simulate potential gains and payouts. In addition, more time will be required to educate the work force about the workings of the metrics. It's simpler to explain one ratio than four or five. However, in the final analysis, most organizations today still prefer the family of measures approach.

Figure 23 on pages 56 and 57 is an example of a family of measures calculation for a garden equipment manufacturing company. The company is privately held and has about 200 employees at one location. All workers are

FIGURE 23: FAMILY OF MEASURES EXAMPLE

Primary Measures

Productivity
Actual Std Hours (Output)		16,000	
Actual Payroll Hours (Input)	33,000		
Baseline x	44.00%		
Expected Std Hours Earned		− 14,520	
Improvement In Std Hours Earned		1,480	
Value Per Hour		x $42.33	
Gain			$62,648

Quality
Units Produced	175,000		
Baseline x	$0.134		
Expected Scrap & Rework		$23,450	
Scrap & Rework — Rolling Average		− $15,000	
Gain			$8,450

(Selected Spending)
Net Sales	$2,500,000		
Baseline x	28.5%		
Expected Spending		$712,500	
Actual Spending		− $650,000	
Gain			$62,500

Total Gain — **$133,598**

Employee Share
Productivity Direct	50%	$31,324
Quality — Scrap/Rework	50%	$4,225
Spending	25%	$15,625
Total Employee Share		**$35,549**
Reserve	50%	$17,775
Monthly Distribution		$17,775
Participating Payroll		$555,000
% Payout		**3.2%**

Current Monthly Reserve	$17,775	
Prior Reserve Accumulation	$65,000	$17,775
Reserve Payout Including Spending		**$82,775**

(Continued)

FIGURE 23: FAMILY OF MEASURES EXAMPLE (CONTINUED)

Special Focus Annual

Safety

Monthly Goal	1	
Number Of Accidents Lost Time	0	
Improvement	1	
Award Per Employee	$30	
Number Of Employees	200	
Monthly Pool		$6,000
Prior Pool Accumulation		$12,000
New Pool Accumulation		**$18,000**

part of the plan, including sales and customer service personnel. The direct productivity measure is based on standard earned hours of output compared to actual payroll hours for production personnel. The spending measure is based on selected spending per dollar of net sales. The selected spending accounts include those that are controllable by employees, including marketing and selling expenses. In addition, selected spending includes the salaries of all office, administration and nonmanufacturing personnel. Wages of manufacturing employees are not included in the spending measure, since hours worked for manufacturing are the input for the productivity measure. Fifty percent of the gain in productivity and quality is shared with employees. The spending measure shares 25 percent of the gain since employee controllability is less than that for productivity and quality. In this example, the monthly bonus is 3.2 percent of participating payroll. Half of the employees' share of the gain is placed in a year-end reserve account, in order to offset deficit months.

There is one special focus pool for safety. Each month that there are no accidents, $30 per employee is placed in an annual pool. If there are two or more accidents in a month, $30 per accident is subtracted from the safety pool accumulation.

Measurement Criteria

After an organization determines the plan's purpose, the distribution group and its position in terms of employee controllability versus common fate, it can begin to zero in on specific measures. Measurement is certainly a major hurdle; however, it is one that organizations always seem to overcome. Most organizations already measure performance in some manner or another. Typically, this is the best place to start. In some cases, the gainsharing measures are straightforward, in other cases they are much more challenging. However, in either case, the organization should test each potential measure against the criteria shown in Figure 24. After brainstorming possible measures and eliminating the obvious, the group discusses each measure in relationship to all of the criteria. In turn, each measure is rated either, "High, Medium or Low" against the criteria.

FIGURE 24: CRITERIA SCREENING TOOL

Category / Measure / Criteria	Productivity			Quality			Service		Safety	
	Lbs/hr	Std hrs to actual hours	Cost/lb	Scrap	Rework	Yield	On-time	Credits	Recordable Accidents	Work Comp
Supports the business	H	H	H	H	H	H	H	H	H	H
Data is readily available	H	H	M	H	H	M	H	H	H	M
Data is accurate	H	H	H	H	H	M	H	H	H	H
Data cannot be unfairly manipulated	H	H	H	H	H	H	H	H	H	H
Employees will trust the numbers	H	M	H	H	H	M	H	H	H	H
Employees can easily understand	H	M	H	H	H	H	H	H	H	H
Employees impact/control	H	H	L	H	M	H	H	H	H	L
More than a few employees can impact	H	H	H	H	H	H	H	H	H	H
Opportunity for improvement	H	H	M	M	H	H	H	H	M	M

Rating Scale: H = High   M = Medium   L = Low

The following are explanations of the chart criteria:

Supports the Business — Whatever is measured must support the business objectives and values. However, I'm not only referring to bottom-line results. A potential measure may be extremely supportive of a company's core values. For example, in the chemical industry, safety is of paramount importance and is inherent to the culture. Some chemical plants go for years without a recordable accident. Even though there is no opportunity for improvement, many chemical plants include recordable accidents as a safety measure. The feeling is that no improvement initiative can be implemented without safety playing an integral part.

Data are accurate — Obviously, the organization cannot reward inaccurate information. As the adage says, "Garbage in, garbage out." Occasionally, an organization may defer gainsharing until some measurement systems are in place. In a few cases, one of the best benefits of gainsharing has been to force companies to develop a comprehensive measurement system. Frequently, the best initial measurements for gainsharing are those already used by the organization.

Data are readily available — Some organizations are able to measure some factors weekly, if not daily. This is particularly true for physical productivity measures. Typically, the more frequent the measure (assuming it is promptly and accurately reported), the greater the awareness and the result. Did you every wonder why a football team looks at the yardage marker on every play?

Data cannot be unfairly manipulated — Gainsharing drives behaviors; however, the system must drive the right behaviors. Are systems in place whereby employees cannot easily misreport results? I know of a brick factory that considered measuring scrap by adding up the daily scrap weight reports from inspectors' batch tickets. The factory decided not to use this measure since there was no method to accurately verify the data.

Will employees readily understand the numbers? — Employees don't necessarily need to understand the detailed math behind all of the calculations. However, employees do need to understand the basics of how the numbers are determined. Some plant accountants argue that a monthly operating variance is the best measure of performance. Operating variance may be important, but will employees understand it? In some cases, regardless of the communications and education efforts, the complexity of the measure does not lend itself to ease of understanding. As one employee told me, "If I can't understand it, how can I trust it?"

Will employees trust the numbers? — Employees may understand the measure, but they may not trust it. This problem typically is a result of "sins from the past." For example, if the organization has a history of reporting, revising and re-reporting a measure, what are the chances that the work force will trust the data, particularly when they're used to drive their bonus?

Can more than a few employees impact the measure? — A measure that is impacted by only a handful of employees typically is not appropriate for gainsharing. It is unwise to attempt to micromanage the measures. Remember, the focus should be on results and not activities. In addition, too many narrow measures can lead to suboptimizing the organization's overall performance. On the other hand, it is unnecessary for everyone in the operation to have a direct impact on the measure. One of my favorite analogies is college basketball. When Michigan State won the national championship, the team was measured by the final score. Everyone on the team, including the players on the bench, trainer and the equipment manager, in some way helped put points up on the board. It wouldn't have made sense to measure the trainer on the number of ankles he or she wrapped. It was a team accomplishment. Everyone, including my next-door neighbor, Phil, the team's optometrist, received a national championship ring.

Do employees impact/control the measure? — To some, controllability is the most important of all the measurement criteria. These criteria are heavily influenced by one's philosophy of gainsharing, the controllability versus the common-fate philosophy. However, even if one's philosophy is common-fate, employees still need to have some control over and influence on the measures. Otherwise, behaviors will not change and at best, the organization will foster an entitlement culture. On the other hand, no matter what the measure, employees will not have 100 percent control of the outcome. There always will be outside factors that people cannot control. That's why I prefer using some historic average as the baseline.

Opportunity for improvement — The opportunity for improvement should be considered. However, it should not necessarily be one of the more important criteria. For example, I have worked with an automobile supplier that measures return parts per million (PPM) parts produced. The PPM rate is almost negligible. However, since PPM performance is of major importance to the company, PPM returns are a gatekeeper measure. This frequent format also is known as a threshold or trigger measurement since it triggers other measurement payouts. No gains from other measures can be shared unless the PPM gate is achieved. Figure 25 represents the measurement model eventually chosen by a design team in a pigment factory.

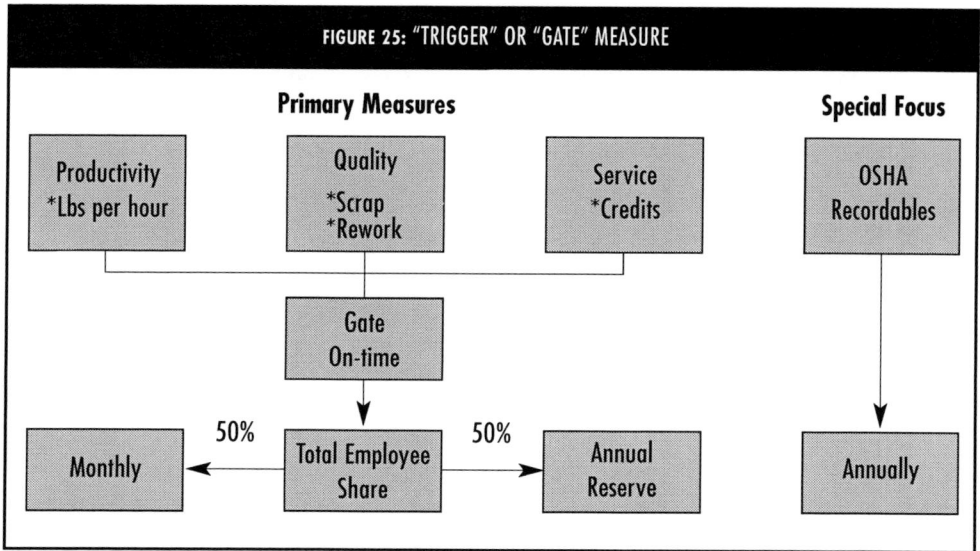

After grouping potential measures into categories of productivity, quality, service and safety, the team decided to pursue six measures. The physical productivity measure of pounds per hour worked was selected primarily because it was rated "High" for all of the criteria. The ratio of standard hours to actual hours was eliminated because the ratio was more difficult to understand and thereby trust. The cost per unit measure was discarded because of the high degree of variability and low control. The measure was a little too broad for the team's liking. In terms of the quality category, scrap and rework were selected. Both directly impact yield (finished pounds/pounds consumed). However, the yield measure only could be measured monthly and was less accurate, therefore representing a potential trust issue.

The service measures were straightforward. The team measured the number of the billing errors per sales dollar and was able to quantify the gain in financial terms. Therefore, credits were counted as a primary measure. On-time shipments were included as a gatekeeper measure. The "green dollar" savings from improved on-time shipments were difficulty to justify. However, on-time shipments were critical to the facility's success. Because of the high impact on the customer, on-time shipments, therefore, were added as a gatekeeper measure.

Finally, OSHA recordables were included in the model as the safety measure. Worker compensation costs were eliminated because a number of outside factors impacted these costs. The plant had a few lingering worker compensation suits from disgruntled employees who had resigned and filed worker comp claims several months later. The team selected OSHA recordables because it was rated "High" for eight of the nine criteria. Safety was treated as a special focus pool, and gains from this measure were to be paid annually and independently from the other measures. The feeling was that "safety is so important that it should stand on its own." The team elected not to reward safety on a monthly basis due to the concern that the facility could have several consecutive payout months with no accidents, and in turn, have horrendous performance for the last few months of the plan year. A monthly payout scheme could potentially generate several payouts in the company's worst safety year on record. Another important point about safety is that the team decided to have the payout reward relatively small for fear of "driving accidents underground."

The pigment company example gives the reader a sense for the company's focus on specific measures. Once measures are carefully screened and organized, the focus can turn to gathering data and preparing a model. Each measure should be charted at least for the most recent 12-month period. Of course a longer time frame would be better.

As the design process continues, the focus turns to methods of valuing gains, employee sharing, reserve accounts and establishing baselines.

In summary, I recall an executive using the analogy of a bulldozer representing a gainsharing plan. The dozer has a number of levers and pedals that control its operations. We push here and step there in order to achieve the desired result. Depending on the job, some levers require more emphasis than others. The levers and pedals for the gainsharing bulldozer are the measures. The measures drive the specific behavior that the organization desires to achieve, whether it is productivity, quality, cost or other organizational goals. Progress must be closely monitored to ensure the end result. Also, modifications in the measures may need to be made over time to reflect changing business conditions, objectives and strategies.

6

Calculation Issues: Values, Sharing and Gatekeepers

Other calculation considerations include how a gain is valued in terms of the green dollar savings. How much of the gain should be shared with employees? Should there be gatekeeper measures? Should any of the gain be set aside for deficit periods? The answers to all the questions are woven together since one impacts the other. Let's first address valuing the gain. How is a gain valued in terms of the green dollar savings?

Valuing the Gain

Perhaps more than any other element in a gainsharing calculation, valuing the gain can have the most significant impact on the dollars to be rewarded. For financial measures, valuing the gain is straightforward; however, valuing gains for physical measures can be more challenging. For example valuing the gain from the multicost ratio (a financial measure) is very direct, per the example in Figure 26.

In Figure 26, the inputs and outputs are both measured in terms of dollars. Given the sales value of production at $5,050,000, the expected costs would be $3,030,000 (60 percent of $5,050,000). However, the actual costs

FIGURE 26: MULTICOST GAIN

Sales Value of Production		$5,050,000
Baseline Ratio (cost/value of production)	x	60%
Expected Costs		$3,030,000
Actual Selected Costs		
Wages and Salaries	$2,020,000	
Utilities	$353,500	
Factory Supplies	$252,500	
Office expenses	+ $50,500	
Total Selected Costs		− $2,676,500
Gain		$353,500

for the period were only $2,676,500. Therefore, it is readily apparent that the gain (or savings) was the difference between the expected and actual, $353,000.

Calculating the gain from a more physical measure is not as straightforward. Once the value has been determined, the number is locked in for the plan year. A common method of valuing a gain is found in the "allowable labor productivity formula" in Figure 27. The output measure is good units and the input measure is labor hours worked. An overzealous manager might want to have overtime hours weighted at $1^1/_2$ time. I certainly wouldn't recommend doing so. What happens if production volume picks up and employees are required to work Saturdays? Most likely there will be a loss, and business conditions may not have been better. Employees would likely complain that they are working harder than ever and are being penalized with the weighting of the hours.

In Figure 27, the baseline productivity ratio is .02 hours per unit or .20 hours per 10 units. Of course, hours could be measured in terms of minutes if it was thought to be more meaningful. In this case, there is a gain because the actual hours worked to produce 1,000,000 good units was less than expected. Since 2,000 fewer hours were used at a value of $15.50 per hour, the gain is calculated to be $31,000. The $15.50 represents the average wages paid to hourly employees during the prior year.

FIGURE 27: ALLOWABLE HOURS FORMULA

Good units	1,000,000		
Baseline Ratio			
Direct hours worked/good unit	x 0.02		
Expected (Allowable) Hours			20,000
Actual Hours Worked		−	18,000
Improvement in Hours			2,000
Average Wages per Hour — Value		x	$15.50
Gain			$31,000

$$\frac{\text{Total annual wages paid to hourly employees}}{\text{Total annual hours worked}} = \frac{\$3,224,000}{208,000} = \$15.50$$

In this case, the gain that is shared represents only the labor cost. In other words, the amount of the gain is a function of the labor rate of $15.50 per hour (2,000 hours x $15.50 = $31,000). Should the $15.50 rate include a "roll-up" for benefits? Should the salaries for supervisors and support staff be added to the $3,224,000 in the calculation? It depends on what the organization believes are the true payroll savings. However, companies tend to include the cost of benefits and support staff in this calculation.

Figure 28 takes a different approach to measuring and valuing the gains in labor productivity. Rather than measure productivity in terms of the allowable labor hours per unit, the productivity ratio has reversed the numerator and denominator. In other words, the productivity ratio is units per hour worked.

FIGURE 28: UNITS PER PAYROLL HOUR FORMULA

Good units				1,000,000
Actual Hours Worked		18,000		
Baseline Ratio				
Units per hour	x	50.00		
Expected (Allowable) Hours				900,000
Improvement in Units			−	100,000
Value per unit			x	$0.60
Gain				$60,000

In this case, the improvement in productivity is the same as in Figure 27. One million units were produced in the same 18,000 hours. However, in this case, the value per unit is $0.60 (valued at total conversion cost: labor, salaries, overhead, utilities, etc). (See Figure 29.)

The only manufacturing cost not included in the value per unit is the cost of raw materials. Therefore, the gain is now valued at $60,000 rather than $31,000. What's the right value? Should a unit be valued at 60 cents (total conversion cost) or only 40 cents for labor and utilities ($0.31 + $0.09)?

FIGURE 29: VALUE PER UNIT

Cost per unit

Labor	$0.31
Salaries	$0.15
Overhead	$0.05
Utilities	$0.09
Total	$0.60

If the organization is working 24-7 and is at production capacity, it could be argued that the productivity gain is total conversion cost ($0.60 per unit).

On the other hand, if the operation is only working one shift at five days a week, one might argue that the gain should be valued at only the labor and utility cost per unit ($0.40 per unit). It comes down to what is fair, and of course, fairness is based upon perceptions. Companies typically should value the gain in terms of the most accurate impact to the bottom line. Top management needs to know the true green dollar impact (savings) of the gain. The issues need to be openly discussed and shared with the team. I remember the comment from a labor relations executive, "I'll never hide a nickel." That was very good advice. The executive played a major role in turning around the adverse labor relations climate in the auto industry in the 1980s.

The method of valuing a gain also ties to the percent of the gain that is shared with employees.

Sharing the Gains

People might think that the amount shared would typically be the most sensitive employee relations issue when designing a plan. However, I have not found this to be the case. When conducting general awareness sessions about the gainsharing concept, I often ask employee groups, "How much should the company share?" If there are no comments, I ask, "How many think 25 percent is fair?" Perhaps 10 percent raise their hand. Then I'll ask, "How many think 50 percent would be fair." In turn, about everyone in the group will raise their hand. However, invariably someone will jokingly shout out, "We should get 100 percent." My typical reply is, "How much would you share if it were your company?" The outspoken employee's friends will chime in, "Zero."

In other words, how much is shared, as well as other gainsharing plan components, has to be fair in the eyes of both company and employees. It gets back to the principle of equity. Both the company and employees must benefit from the plan.

The most common single sharing percent is 50 percent to employees and 50 percent to the company. The reason a 50/50 split is so frequently used is basically that it sounds fair. How can you argue the point? The most common range of sharing is between 25 percent and 50 percent. However, there are a few cases in which the employee share percent is as low as 5 percent or as high as 100 percent.

The following are points to consider in determining the appropriate sharing percent.

Appropriate Level of Award for Appropriate Level of Performance

One common approach is to work the numbers backward. In other words, what percentage bonus is appropriate for outstanding, good and satisfactory levels of improvement? Of course, it depends on the organization and the business environment. A company in a survival mode would have a different view than a company that is in a more comfortable competitive environment. However, Figure 30 may provide a general rule of thumb.

FIGURE 30: STANDARD BONUS SCALE

Performance Level	Bonus % of Total Comp
Best Demonstrated	16% and above
Outstanding	11% – 15%
Good	6% – 10%
Satisfactory	3% – 5%

The performance level, "best demonstrated," basically is saying that if an organization looks at each measure by month, and assuming that this level of performance could be maintained for 12 months, what would be the potential payout? When this scenario was recently applied to a company in Spain, the total annual gain was calculated to be $1,531,000, $412,000 of which would be shared with employees. The bonus amount calculated to be 22 percent of annual compensation. The operations general manager thought the result was great for everyone involved, "The bigger the gainsharing bonus, the greater the gain for the company."

For the long haul, if payouts are in the 4 percent to 5 percent range, employee focus and interest can be maintained. However, it all comes down to employee expectations. Employees who have been given the impression that they will need "wheelbarrows to haul away all their gains" certainly will be disappointed. It always is best to explain gainsharing's benefits in terms of improved employee involvement, communications and teamwork. A case in point involved a company that implemented separate gainsharing plans at two of its plants located in Texas. The facilities were only about four miles apart. In the first year, payouts were about the same in both facilities, about

2.5 percent of compensation. A follow-up gainsharing monitoring survey was conducted at both facilities one year after the plans were implemented. The survey findings were much different for the two plants. Figure 31 compares the findings on survey items related to the bonus calculation.

FIGURE 31: COMPARISON OF TWO FACILITIES

SCALE

1	2	3	4	5
Strongly Disagree	Disagree	Neither Agree nor Disagree	Agree	Strongly Agree

The Bonus Calculation	Laporte	Deer Park	% Difference
1. I see a relationship between the work I do and the amount of bonus earned.	2.9	3.7	22%
2. I understand what things are included in the bonus calculation.	3.4	3.8	11%
3. I understand how the bonus calculation works.	3.2	3.8	16%
4. I feel that the bonus calculation is fair.	3.1	4.0	23%

At the Deer Park facility, employees were very positive about their gainsharing plan. Employees commented positively that their gainsharing plan helped foster improved teamwork and communications. However, employees in the second facility complained about their gainsharing plan's fairness and amount of their bonus. They had very little good to say about the plan. Managers at the second facility initially introduced gainsharing in terms of an incentive, "bonus" plan rather than an employee involvement initiative.

Measurement philosophy — When organizations have a broad calculation such as the multicost approach, the sharing percent typically is less than if the measure was based on a narrower, labor-only calculation. When a multicost formula is used, a company may share perhaps only 25 percent of the gain. In the multicost approach, a company is sharing in a number of the costs: labor, energy, overhead, etc. Some of these costs may be driven by the company's investment in equipment and capital. For example, if the cost of raw materials were included in the formula, why should the company share 50 percent of the gain? After all, the company is buying the materials and purchasing the energy. The company, not the employee, is taking the risk. Shouldn't the company get a larger share? On the other hand, if the formula is a labor-only measure, companies share a greater percentage, generally 50 percent to 75 percent of the gain. Why? In a labor-only formula, the company only shares the gains in labor cost. Logically, employees should receive a larger percent of the gain associated with their efforts. In a labor-only calculation, for every additional unit produced at the same amount of labor, the company shares only the labor cost per unit. In this case, the company receives 100 percent of the gain in all nonlabor costs associated with producing an additional unit.

Controllability and importance — When organizations use a family of measures approach, the sharing percent may vary depending on the measure. Those measures that are more important to the company and are more controllable by employees will have a larger sharing percentage. If quality is No. 1, why not share 50 percent? On the other hand, if productivity is second to quality, it would be a powerful message to share 40 percent to perhaps 30 percent of the productivity gain.

Variable share — In some cases, an organization may decide to have a variable sharing percent. At lower levels of improvement, the sharing percent may be relatively small. As performance improves, the sharing level is increased. This approach was used at a Sylvania lighting components factory. The plant was facing severe competition from foreign sources. The future was not particularly bright. The family of measures approach was utilized. A major measure was manufacturing cost per net sales. The dilemma: if 30 percent of the gain was shared above the historical level of performance, the facility potentially could pay out a substantial bonus and still remain noncompetitive. On the other hand, if a baseline was set at a more competitive cost to sales ratio, the likelihood of a payout in the first plan year was rather remote. In addition, like many other facilities, the plant had a large number of "nay sayers." Most likely, after the first six months of gainsharing, many workers would say, "See, I told you it would never work. Costs have come down, but the company isn't sharing a nickel of the savings." Faced with this vexing problem, the plant established a baseline using the prior 12 months' history of selected cost to sales. In addition, a more aggressive target cost to sales ratio was established. Ten percent of the gain was shared at performance levels above the historical baseline, and 30 percent of the gain was shared for improvement above the target. As a result, the plant experienced some early positive quarters. The payouts were small, but employee confidence in the plan gradually increased. Employee interest in the plan also grew, which in turn yielded better performance improvements. As one of the design team members said, "How can a pole-vaulter jump 15 feet if he has never jumped 10?"

Gatekeeper Measures

As previously mentioned, occasionally, certain measures may be assigned the role of a gatekeeper. In other words, before a gain in one measure (or multiple measures) can be shared, the gain first must be qualified by meeting a minimum level of acceptable performance in another measure. A good example is a gate adopted by an automotive supplier. The factory had an excellent reputation of providing quality parts to its customers as measured by the number of customer-returned parts per million parts shipped. In fact, parts returned per million were so few that there was little opportunity for improvement. On the other hand, the factory had a significant opportunity to improve its productivity. Therefore, it was possible that employees, in their quest to seek substantial productivity gains, could potentially "push parts out the door" at the expense of increasing the number of returns. In fact, a measurement simulation disappointedly demonstrated that a 10 percent improvement in productivity and 50 percent worse performance in returns could net a handsome bonus. Therefore, to correct the problem, returned parts per million parts shipped was used as a gatekeeper measure. If, in a given month, the parts per million gate was not achieved, the employee share of the productivity gain would be deferred to the end of the plan year. If the parts per million year-end goal was achieved, the deferred gain would be paid. However, if the year-end goal was not achieved, employees would forfeit the deferred dollars. In other words, if employees had a bad month in terms of customer returns, they shouldn't give up; they should stay focused on the year-end parts per million goal.

If a gatekeeper measure is used, organizations need to clearly recognize that the purpose of the gate is to prevent performance in a very important measure from deteriorating. Consider the analogy of a fence around a factory's property. The fence is for security. When people pass through the gate, they open it and walk through. People typically don't jump over gates. Therefore, a gate shouldn't be a stretch to achieve. Typically, historical data should set the gate.

Also, a gate usually should be a measure that has a historically consistent degree of employee controllability. If the payment of gains is based on qualifying through a single measure, employees should have a relatively high degree of control and trust in the measure. A gatekeeper measure sends a very powerful message. In the automotive supplier example it says, "The customer is No. 1."

Occasionally, organizations use profitability as a gatekeeper measure. Of course, the line of sight of profits is very distant. An organization using a profitability gate clearly would be adopting the common-fate measurement philosophy. One company that uses a profit gate is SGS Tool Company of Munroe Falls, Ohio. SGS is a family-owned company with approximately 350 employees. The company enjoys a relatively high degree of employee identity to the organization and its overall success. The level of worker loyalty is exemplified by low employee turnover and long service. When the SGS design team prioritized the gainsharing plan's goals, the team's No. 1 goal was to keep the company profitable, strong and competitive. Employees clearly recognized their common fate with the company's success. Even though the plan has a family of measures approach, a return-on-assets gate is used. Basically, the calculation focused on line-of-sight measures (productivity, scrap, spending and customer service). However, no quarterly gain can be paid unless a minimum return-on-assets gate is met. To further reinforce the common-fate philosophy, the sharing percent increases as the company's return on assets improves.

7

Baseline Consideration: Setting the Bar

There are many causes for failure of a gainsharing plan. One of the more common ones relates to establishing an overly aggressive baseline. If the baseline is not perceived to be fair, gainsharing clearly can become a de-motivator. The baseline decision can undo everything that an organization has attempted to do by implementing gainsharing in the first place. Unfortunately, I commonly find that when initially exploring gainsharing, employee trust in management is far from positive. Trust issues often have been aggravated by failures of past performance-improvement initiatives. Employees often comment about the "program-of-the-month syndrome." A poorly executed gainsharing plan, since money is potentially involved, can have an especially adverse impact on trust.

A common gainsharing calculation questions is, "How do we set the baseline? If we set it too low, the company could pay out for false gains. If we set it too high, people might get discouraged and give up." Setting the baseline is influenced by a number of factors: technology, business conditions, organizational culture and gainsharing philosophy.

Generally, there are three common approaches to setting the initial baseline: history, target or a combination of both.

History

By far, establishing a baseline at some historical average level of performance is the most common approach. History has a number of advantages over using targeted (or budgeted) level of performance as the baseline. First, employees typically trust history. This is particularly true if an operation has regularly measured and shared performance data. The numbers are the actual results. History is what it is.

Using history as the baseline also gives employees confidence that they have a chance at getting over the bar. For example, as shown in Figure 32, if the prior 12-month period is used, in most cases, the organization has demonstrated that it could get over the bar six of 12 attempts.

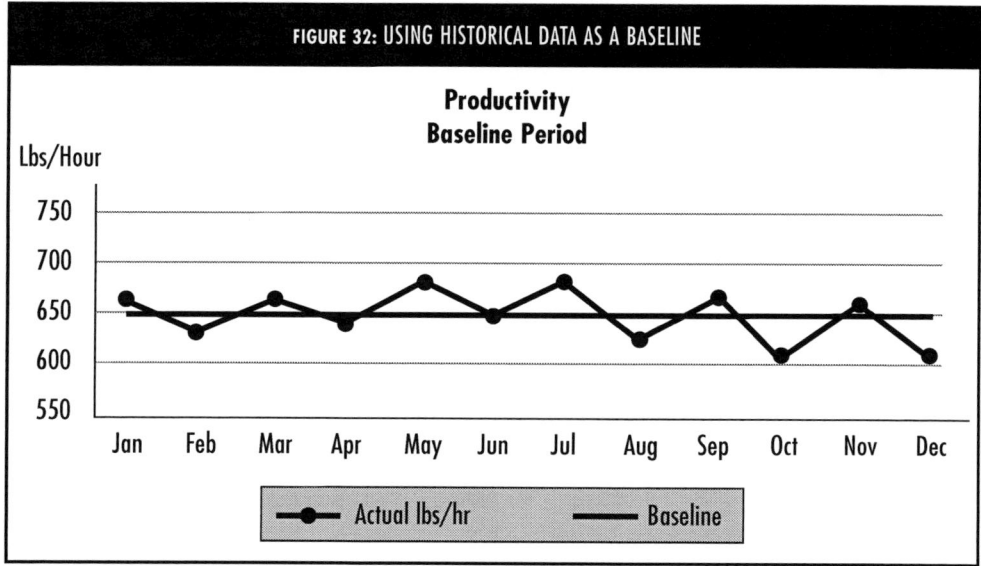

FIGURE 32: USING HISTORICAL DATA AS A BASELINE

Most employees recognize that they can learn from mistakes and that better communications and teamwork will help generate gains. As gains are shared, confidence will grow, and improved confidence builds better performance.

No matter the measure, employees will not have 100 percent control of the outcome. If history is used as the baseline, history automatically accounts for factors influencing the measures that are outside of employees' and the organization's control. Assuming that uncontrolled or unforeseen events will occur in the future, the baselines most likely will be perceived as fair.

By far the most important argument for using history as a baseline is that it reinforces the need for change. If the organization repeats historical performance, there will be no gain. The company needs to change. Basically, the organization is the people. Therefore, for there to be a gain, people need to do things differently than they have in the past. People have to change their behaviors. Many employees may point at management, another department or the need for co-workers to change. However, the dilemma is that one person cannot generally "change another." As the adage states, "You can lead a horse to water, but you can't make it drink." People need to recognize that they need to change themselves; pointing fingers at someone else will not lead to gains. If a minority of the organization changes, gains will be generated and shared with everyone. As gains are shared, the "fence sitters" gradually become "go-getters," and greater gains will result.

If a baseline is set *above* a historical average, gainsharing will have much more difficulty in promoting organizational change.

If history is used, then exactly how much history should be used? Gainsharing plans from yesteryear often used at least two- or three-year historical data to develop the baseline. Today, with rapidly changing business conditions, most organizations would find that a baseline period of two years typically would be too long. Seasonality and other business cycle factors are built into the baseline. Generally, I prefer to use the most recent 12-month period as the baseline. Most organizations have somewhat of an annual business cycle; therefore, a 12-month period will even things out. On occasions in which seasonal factors are dramatic, "smoothing" or other measurement techniques are used to remove the variability of the calculation.

Target as the Baseline

On occasion, historical data is not appropriate for establishing the baseline. This is particularly true in new operations or operations that have recently installed new equipment or technology, or when an industry is in a major state of flux. In these cases, a rolling baseline sometimes is utilized. For example, if a plan had a quarterly payout frequency, the baseline might adjust every quarter by averaging the three previous quarters of performance as the new baseline. Therefore, a new baseline would be calculated each quarter. The rolling average process would continue until the baseline achieved a targeted level of performance. At that point, the baseline would remain fixed for the duration of the plan year. Typically, the rolling average would exclude quarters that were below the previous baseline. Otherwise, the organization could be rewarding for worse performance. Companies find this approach helpful since it rewards employees for getting a new operation up and running as soon as possible. The approach is more credible than basing gains on performance of a targeted number, which often is a guess. (See Figure 33.)

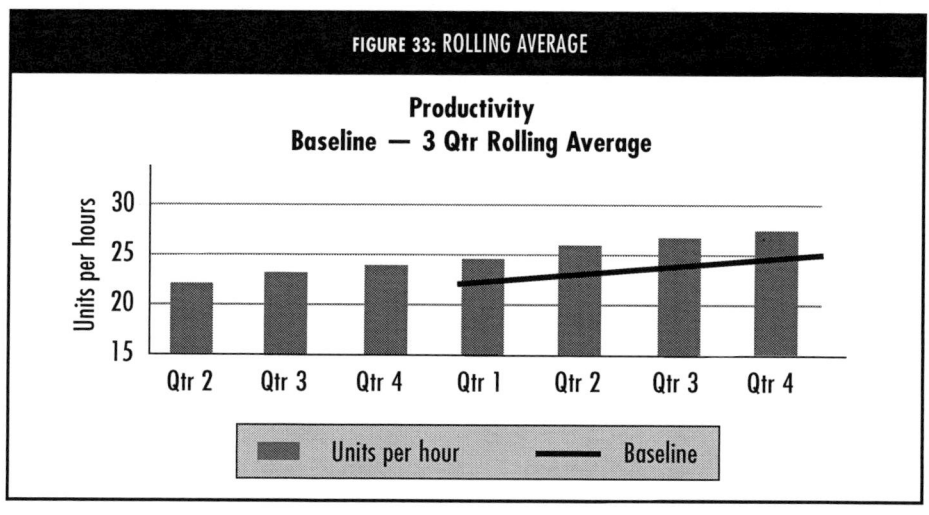

Also, a targeted baseline might make sense for a facility that is fighting for survival in a severely competitive environment. In this type of scenario, a company may not be in a position to have payouts for small improvements above historical performance. As discussed earlier, a variable share approach might be appropriate for a facility in a survival mode. In other words, a low level of sharing for performance above a historical baseline and a greater level of sharing for targeted performance. (See Figure 34.)

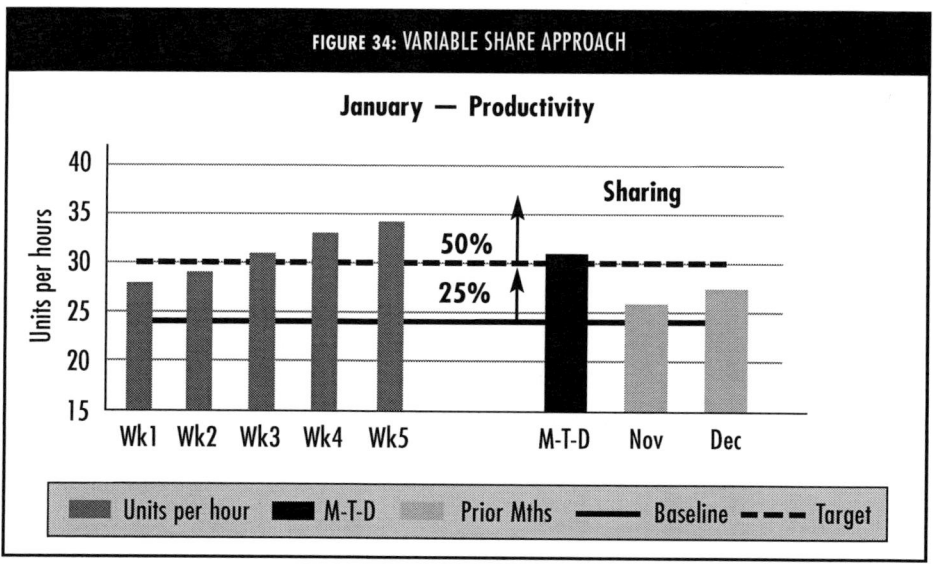

Regardless, when a target is used as the baseline, the organization has to determine the level of performance that is appropriate before a gain will be shared. Of course, whatever is done, the baseline must be perceived as fair. More discussion and education will be necessary to assure understanding. A targeted baseline approach requires a higher level of organizational trust and might not be suitable for many cultures.

Beware of using a budget as the baseline. Basically, a budget is a target. It looks at historical data when it is being established. However, a budget often is massaged and negotiated with upper management. For some companies, managers find the budgeting process to be very trying and stressful. In some cultures, it would be hard to imagine that lower-level employees would understand how the baseline number was established, let alone to trust and perceive that the baseline is fair. I recall a lighting plant in Kentucky that insisted on using a baseline of budget. After about nine months of no gains, the work force was completely demoralized.
On the other hand, a neighboring facility used a baseline equal to the prior year's performance. This facility made initial gains and did progressively better as it gained confidence in the plan.

Baseline Adjustments

Traditional gainsharing plans had fixed baselines with the baseline remaining the same from one plan year to the next. If baselines were adjusted over time, companies would "buy out" the old baseline by providing some form of added compensation. The added compensation or bonus would represent some percentage of the value of the employee share of a gain between the higher baseline and the old fixed baseline. However, today, gainsharing plans generally call for and annually review an adjustment of the baseline(s). The reason again is due to the rapidly changing business conditions and improving technology.

Moreover, in today's competitive environment, the baseline must be increased. A portion of a company's share of the gains are indirectly passed onto the customer in terms of price reductions, improved quality and better customer service. As shown in Figure 35 on page 81, if a baseline remains fixed from plan year to plan year, the gains passed onto the customer would erode the company's share. However, employees would continue to receive

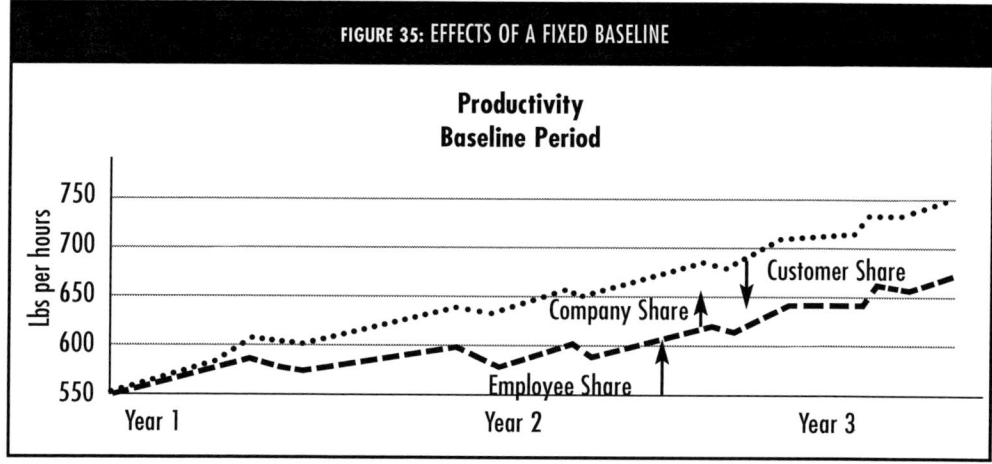

FIGURE 35: EFFECTS OF A FIXED BASELINE

their full share. In the extreme, a company could be pushed into a losing proposition. Obviously, the result would be the demise of the company and the gainsharing plan.

One might think that employees would object to an annual adjustment of the baseline. However, in today's world, most employees understand the need for continuous improvement — and indeed should come to expect an annual adjustment because the company has communicated it clearly from the onset. The issue is not whether the baseline *should* change, but *how* should it change? One approach would be to simply review the issue at the end of each plan year, per the following plan provision statement:

> **Adjustments of the Baseline:** After the first plan year, and each year thereafter, the baselines used in the calculation will be reviewed and adjusted by management and the design team.

Most likely, management would prefer this approach because it gives it maximum flexibility on the baseline adjustment. Unfortunately, the provision is nebulous and would require a relatively high level of organizational trust. There is nothing to say that a company might get "greedy" and aggressively increase the baseline following the first plan year. A number of employees might argue, "Why should we work harder or smarter, if the company is going to turn around and take all the gain from us next year?"

Therefore, it is best to have a clearly defined methodology for future baseline adjustments. As stated previously, the procedure should be developed and clearly communicated when the gainsharing plan is initially implemented. So, how should the baseline change? It depends primarily on the type of business, the plan measures and the competitive business climate.

A labor-intensive business most likely would adjust a baseline more gradually than a business that is more capital intensive. A company that adopts physical/operational measures would adjust the baseline more aggressively than an organization that utilizes broader, more financial measures. The more the measure moves toward profits, the less aggressive the baseline adjustment. In fact, if an organization adopts a measure that parallels profit-sharing, the baseline may remain fixed. A company that is in serious financial trouble will need to be more aggressive in the baseline adjustment.

One simple solution would be to adjust the new plan year's baseline to the average of the prior plan year's performance, as shown in Figure 36.

This approach would not be typical since the baseline would be ratcheted up very quickly. In this scenario, employees could make a good argument that the company will receive the benefits of the improvements for years to come. On the other hand, employees will only benefit from the improvement for the initial plan year. Another argument is that if the baseline is ratcheted up by the prior year's full improvement, payouts will dramatically decline,

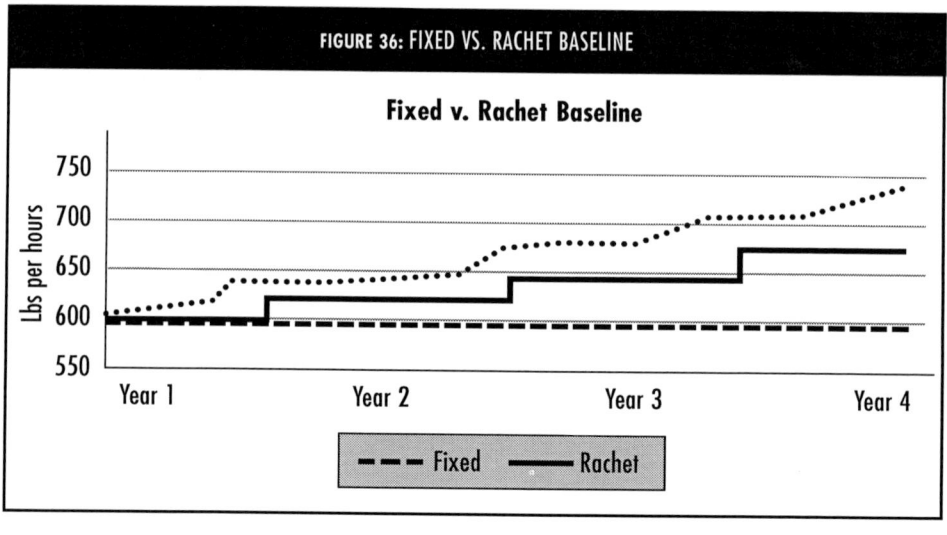

FIGURE 36: FIXED VS. RACHET BASELINE

and the plan will quickly "burn out." Therefore, I typically recommend that the baseline move up but on a more gradual year-to-year basis. A common approach is to have a new year's baseline adjusted on the basis of the most recent three years. (See Figure 37 for an example.)

FIGURE 37: BASELINE ADJUSTMENTS

Plan year		Baseline periods
Initial plan year	=	Prior 12 month period
2nd plan year	=	Average (initial baseline and 1st plan year results)
3rd plan year	=	Average (initial baseline + 1st plan year + 2nd plan year)
4th plan year	=	Average (1st plan year + 2nd plan year + 3rd plan year)
Subsequent years	=	Average of prior three years

In this example, the baseline adjustment provides employees the opportunity to receive a portion of the first year's gains over the following three-year period. However, the continuous improvement concept is still being reinforced. This approach would be reasonable for a successful facility that utilizes the family of measures approach. An example of this approach is used by a facility in western Kentucky. The facility is relatively modern with a high degree of automation and is in a fairly capital-intensive industry. It has six gainsharing measures; however, the productivity measure has the highest potential for generating gains. Productivity is measured in terms of pounds per hour worked. When productivity gains are calculated, the value per unit is based on total conversion cost, which is about three times the value, as if a pound was only valued at labor cost per pound.

Conversely, if an operation has perhaps a more narrow measure, such as allowable labor per unit of output, the baseline adjustments may be less aggressive. An organization may use a weighted averaging approach. (See Figure 38 on page 84.) In this case, the later years are given more weight than the most recent year's performance. As discussed earlier, an allowable labor formula values productivity gains only in terms of the labor cost. If the gains were only valued at labor cost, the baseline adjustment would be less aggressive. For each additional unit of output at the same amount of labor input, the company benefits by its share of the labor cost per unit, as well as reaping 100 percent of the non-labor cost per unit.

FIGURE 38: BASELINE ADJUSTMENTS WITH LESS AGGRESSIVE WEIGHTED AVERAGING APPROACH

Plan year	Weighted avg.		Prior 12-month period	Results year 1		Results year 2		Results year 3		
Initial plan year	=		1							
2nd plan year	=		2	x	1					
3rd plan year	=		3	x	2	x	1			
4th plan year	=				3	x	2	x	1	
Subsequent years	=		Weighting sequence continues							

An aluminum extrusion company used the weighted average approach for its three factories. The company's factory operations are more labor intensive than the facility in western Kentucky. The approach has proven to be successful for both the company and employees. The plan has been in place for several years.

Finally, a company in a survival mode may increase the baseline more aggressively, since many of the gains need to be indirectly passed onto the customer in the form of price concessions. In this case, the weighting sequence may be reversed; a more recent year's performance would receive a greater weight. An automotive after-market supplier used this more aggressive approach. The baseline is adjusted annually by using the most recent three-year average. However, the best year is weighted three times, the second best, two times, and the third, one time.

Whatever the methodology, it is important to have an understanding that worst performance typically will not be added to the new baseline. For example, if the performance in plan year 2 is worse than the current baseline, plan year 2's actual performance would not be included in the new baseline adjustment. However, on occasion, baselines may be lowered due to process changes, product mix or other business conditions that support a lowering of the baseline.

I can't emphasize enough that regardless of the method employed, the baseline adjustment must be perceived as fair for both employees and the company. In one company, there was no upfront methodology spelled out for how the baseline would be changed. After a highly successful first year, the facility was overly aggressive in setting the new baseline. The bar for productivity increased by approximately 20 percent. In the second plan year, the company continued to gain from the previous operating improvements; however, the payouts dramatically declined. A follow-up employee survey confirmed that trust levels in the organization had plummeted.

Mid-Year Baseline Adjustments

It is highly recommended that organizations have a gainsharing plan provision that recognizes that it may be necessary to adjust the baseline midyear to account for a significant investment in capital or technology. Added capital could have a significant impact on the calculated gains. Employees certainly would like to have the full benefits, but the plan needs to be fair for the company. After all, the investors need to see a return from the investment in capital. In part, this problem is overcome by the annual adjustment of the baseline. Some organizations recognizing this are comfortable to proceed without a mid-year adjustment. However, it is best to have an upfront understanding that it may be necessary to adjust the baseline midyear. The following is an example for such a plan provision:

> **Capital:** Though not common, management may make midyear baseline adjustments to reflect capital improvements. It is recognized that future capital investments or changes in technology could directly impact some of the performance measures. It is further recognized that the company needs to recover the gains from capital as soon as possible. In the event of a significant capital investment, management will meet with the design team and discuss the impact on the current and future baselines.

Occasionally, organizations may take a more specific approach by specifying a dollar investment level that triggers a mid-year baseline change. Of course the dollar level will vary with the size and type of operations. In addition, the plan may be specific as to when the adjustment will be made. In other words, how long after the investment is made before the baseline is adjusted? Some organizations may only make a partial adjustment to the baseline when capital is installed (the argument being that everyone's support for the new project is necessary, and employees should receive some of the benefit).

A brick factory in Missouri utilized this more specific approach. If $100,000 or more were invested in new equipment, the baseline would be re-evaluated after a four-month startup and debugging period. As an incentive to employees, the baseline would only be adjusted by 80 percent of the total input of the capital. However, the specificity in this example is more the exception than the rule. The trust levels were relatively low at the Missouri factory before gainsharing was implemented.

In other cases, plant managers have used gainsharing as a tool to reward the prompt and successful startup of new equipment. Managers have identified and set a date as a goal for getting new equipment "debugged" and fully operational. In turn, if the goal is achieved, employees are rewarded a "little added bonus" to their gainsharing checks. Also, if the equipment goes online sooner, employees will reap the financial benefits of the productivity improvement before the baseline is adjusted.

Another approach is to use a transitional baseline to encourage employees to assist in the installation and startup of new capital. The transitional baseline is used for a temporary period during the startup process. The approach uses a combination of history and target to calculate a moving baseline. Once the targeted level of performance is attained, the baseline will return to the annual baseline methodology.

A plastics coloring plant in St. Peters, Mo. used a transitional approach. As the St. Peters gainsharing plan was being designed, the company announced a major reconfiguration of its manufacturing operation. As a result, equipment from other company plants was to be moved and re-installed at St. Peters. The reconfiguration also required St. Peters to add building space and move some existing equipment. Because of the disruption, one alternative was to put the implementation of the gainsharing plan on hold until the plant was reconfigured and debugged. Instead, the facility decided to move forward with gainsharing and have a transitional baseline. The plan language for St. Peters' transitional baseline is as follows:

> Plant modernization: For the first plan year, the plant will be adding and removing production lines. In order to encourage an efficient transition, fair and equitable baselines must be established for each new line. Therefore, the following methodology will be followed for the conversion:
>
> During the startup period, a new line (first three months of production) will have a *targeted* baseline. The plant manager will set the target. During the three-month transition, if the target is exceeded, a gain will be calculated. In the event that there is a loss, the loss will be forgiven.
>
> After the transition period, a three-month rolling average baseline will be applied as follows: For the fourth month after the transition, a baseline will be established based on the prior three months' average. For subsequent months, the baseline will be based on a three-month rolling average (current month plus the prior two months). However, in no event will the baseline be eased.

The St. Peters plan has a monthly payout frequency with a reserve for deficit months. During the transition period, if performance should fall below the baseline, the loss would be forgiven and not charged against the year-end reserve account. Employees saw the approach as being very fair.

Organizations that invest in capital heavily on an ongoing basis or those in a rapid growth mode might consider a rolling average baseline rather than a baseline that is fixed for a full plan year. For example, an organization might have a 24-month rolling baseline. If the payout frequency were monthly, the baseline for a given month would represent the average of the prior 24 months. In this case, the need for a mid-year baseline adjustment would not be necessary. However, in the long run, this approach might generate relatively small payouts, and in turn, generate less employee enthusiasm for the plan. I haven't found many organizations that utilize the rolling baseline approach, usually because employees don't trust an ever-changing target.

Regardless of how the capital issue is addressed, the issue needs to be thoroughly discussed and communicated before the plan becomes effective. Again, the best advice is to do what is fair for both the company and employees.

8

Frequency of Payout, Minimum Payout and Reserve Account Frequency

The majority of today's plans provide for either a monthly or quarterly payout frequency. There are a few plans today that may provide payout opportunities as frequent as weekly and as infrequent as annually. Generally, I highly discourage an annual payout frequency. Those that have an annual payout system typically are unhappy with the result. I find that monthly or quarterly works best. So, what's better, monthly or quarterly?

Often, the frequency of reinforcement offered by a monthly payout system yields better results than a quarterly system, particularly during the initial year of the plan. Obviously, a quarterly system provides the opportunity of increasing the magnitude of a bonus check. However, as one manager commented, "We prefer monthly rather than quarterly, because it gives us 12 opportunities to celebrate rather than four. Remember, the payout is the score."

Generally, the measure and type of work force drive the decision on the frequency of payout. Some measures are not suitable for a monthly payout frequency due to the variability of the data. For example, if spending were a monthly measure, the timing of when a bill is paid or received would impact the gain or loss.

Also, the makeup of the work force can influence the payout frequency. A work force consisting primarily of manual laborers or one that has a high level of turnover may find a weekly or monthly system more appropriate. On the other hand, a hospital having a work force of trained professionals may be better suited for a quarterly system. I am working with an equipment development company that pays some measures semiannually and others annually. The work force consists of professional and engineering personnel.

Minimum Payout

I'll never forget one company stating that it chose to have its gainsharing paid annually because a neighboring facility had a monthly system and found its employees were insulted when the first monthly bonus "was only $2.50."

Having an annual system was not the answer; all that was needed was a minimum payout level. If a monthly gain does not meet the minimum bonus criteria, it is deferred to the next period. If the minimum is never achieved, the gain is paid at year-end.

On the other hand, I had a design team in Arizona decide that the minimum monthly payout should be $100. The facility went almost a full year before it had a payout. There was little interest in the plan. The design team failed to understand that initial gains have a tendency to be small and increase as awareness and understanding is developed. An early payout of $25 may have gotten the attention of at least 50 percent of the workers. The result would have been larger future gains and a better first year.

The Reserve Account

I'm always surprised to learn that some gainsharing plans have a monthly or quarterly payout frequency with no provision for a reserve to recover deficit periods. A year-end reserve account basically assures consequences for poor performance and helps reinforce longer-term thinking.

Figure 39 gives an example of a quarterly payout frequency with no annual reserve. Of course, the actual numbers would be much larger than those in the example. A gain in one quarter is offset by a loss in the next. Therefore, when considering the full year, there is a zero gain. On the other hand, when there is a positive quarter, 50 percent of the quarterly gain is shared with employees. There are no consequences for bad performance. In the example, employees receive a bonus for two quarters, totaling $70 for the full year. Employees certainly are not going to pay back the $70. If there is no gain for the year and the owner just paid out $70, he actually lost $70. Bad deal for the company owner!

FIGURE 39: EFFECT OF VARIABILITY

	Quarter				
	1st	2nd	3rd	4th	Full Year
Total Gain	$100	($100)	$40	($40)	$0
Employee Share (50%) Payout	$50	–	$20	–	$70

How should the owner design the plan to avoid the problem? One answer would be to increase the baseline. Bad idea. Using the analogy of the pole-vaulter, if the bar is too high, the pole-vaulter will quickly become discouraged and demoralized. Another alternative would be for the owner to pay out annually. In this case, the pole-vaulter is rewarded once per year. With only annual recognition, how much interest will the pole-vaulter have in competing? The answer is, obviously, very little.

The best answer is to use a reserve account to help offset deficit periods. Figure 40 is an example of the typical reserve account mechanics.

In the example, for each positive quarter, 50 percent of the employees' share of the gain is held in a reserve account. In the event of a loss, the full amount of the employees' share of the loss is used to offset the reserve. At the end of the year, a positive reserve is distributed to all eligible participants. If the year-end reserve balance is negative, the owner absorbs the loss. The reserve then begins anew the next plan year. In this scenario, there was no gain and only $35 rather than $70 was paid. Nevertheless, the owner still has a loss; however, the amount was minimized. I should point out that this scenario is very rare. Basically a negative reserve is a sign of a failing gainsharing plan.

Occasionally someone will argue for a loss recovery reserve. In other words, no quarterly payouts are made until a loss in the reserve is recovered. For

FIGURE 40: DEFICIT RESERVE

	Quarter				
	1st	2nd	3rd	4th	Full Year
Total Gain	$100	($100)	$40	($40)	$0
Employee Share (50%)	$50	($50)	$20	($20)	
Withheld for Reserve (50%)	$25	($50)	$10	($20)	
Paid out Employee	$25	–	$10	–	$35
Reserve Balance	$25	($25)	($15)	($35)	

example, in Figure 40, the reserve balance in the second quarter was minus $25. In the third quarter, the employee share was plus $20 and the third quarter's payout was $10. However, if there were a full loss recovery, the third quarter payout would be zero. Why? Because the employee share of the gain ($20) was not enough to recover the $25 deficit in the reserve account. However, I discourage the loss recovery approach. Imagine a pole-vaulter looking at a bar 10-foot high (his average jump), and the coach digs a three-foot hole in the runway. How high does the pole vaulter have to jump now? Thirteen feet. Unfortunately, his prior record was 11 feet. Gainsharing plans have a tendency to get off to a slow start. Remember, we are dealing with changing behavior. Obviously, this doesn't happen overnight. If a facility starts with an initial loss, employees may feel that they may never recover, even though the loss is not necessarily the fault of the reserve system, but may have been caused by poor design and implementation.

Someone else may have a good argument that if the reserve is negative at the end of the plan year, the negative balance should be carried over to the next plan year. Some plans do this, but I think it is another bad idea. How would a football team feel if it had to start a new season with three losses before it played even one game?

As previously noted, the reserve is intended to reinforce longer-term thinking. An organization is always going to have its bad periods. The objective of the reserve is to minimize the loss. Figure 41 (next page) provides a good example of the impact of minimizing the deficit.

In this example, instead of giving up in the second quarter, employees protect the reserve by holding the loss to a minus $10. In the second quarter, the employees' share of the loss is minus $5 ($10 x 50 percent). Therefore, the second quarter's reserve balance now is positive $20. In the example, the reserve remains positive for the balance of the plan year. The positive reserve balance generated a year-end bonus of $10. By minimizing the loss in the second quarter, there is a total gain of $90, and the total employee share is $45 ($35 +$10).

How much of the gain should be held back in the reserve? It depends on the measures and the payout frequency. If the measures are ones that are relatively stable from quarter to quarter, the reserve will be a smaller share of the employee's gain. If the payout period is more frequent, the reserve will be more. The reserve for a monthly plan frequently may be 50 percent and a quarterly plan 25 percent.

FIGURE 41: DEFICIT RESERVE

	Quarter				
	1st	2nd	3rd	4th	Full Year
Total Gain	$100	($10)	$40	($40)	$90
Employee Share (50%)	$50	($5)	$20	($20)	
Withheld for Reserve (50%)	$25	($5)	$10	($20)	
Paid out Employee	$25	–	$10	–	$35
Reserve Balance	$25	$20	$30	$10	$10

Moreover, the reserve account can have significant motivational value as it grows through the plan year. As the reserve grows, organizations use a variety of interesting techniques to promote its potential. One of the more unique ways of promoting the reserve was used by a plant manager in a facility of approximately 100 people. The gainsharing plan distributed 50 percent of the employees' share of the gain monthly and the second half of the employees' share was placed in a year-end reserve account. For the first plan year, the plant manager set a goal of having a reserve of $100,000 or $1,000 per employee. The plant manager had monthly meetings with all employees to announce the bonus results. Since the plan was new, employees failed to understand the magnitude of the reserve. After the first six months, the reserve had accumulated to $50,000 or about $500 per person. In the monthly meeting, the plant manager took 500 $1 bills and as he explained the reserve, he threw the $500 into the air. Clearly, the manager grabbed everyone's attention. Notably, at the end of the plan year, the reserve accumulated to $160,000, averaging $1,600 per person.

9

Method of Distribution

The method of distributing the gain among the plan participants is by far the most controversial issue in terms of a gainsharing plan's design. In other words, if the employees' share of the gain is $10,000, how is the money distributed to the participants? The basic options are: 1) equal share, 2) equal percentage or 3) equal cents per hour. All of these alternatives are "equal." However, the meaning of "equal" will be different for different people. The issue deals with a person's sense of fairness. The problem is that one person's view of fair can be completely different from another person's view. It all comes down to perceptions. There is no right answer. At times, a person's view of fairness can become quite emotional.

Most managers and executives also have a strong opinion on this issue; however, management can find itself in a quagmire if it attempts to make the decision. After all, it's the employee's share. Why should management decide? Clearly, the design team should make this decision. Regardless, not everyone will be happy. However, I have found that the decision does not make or break a plan.

A word of caution: I discourage going down the path of distributing the gain in a manner that attempts to recognize individual performance. It generally doesn't make sense to say, "Here are the gains we generated by working together, and we'll give Charlie more because his performance rating is higher than Sue's." Other compensation plans can address individual performance.

Three basic alternatives for distributing the gains are listed in Figure 42 on page 97.

Equal Share — Historically, the equal share method is the most common method of distributing the gains. The method is the most supportive of the gainsharing philosophy. Basically, it says that we all contribute together, and we, therefore, share together. It doesn't make a difference in terms of one's position in the company, his/her compensation level or the number of hours

FIGURE 42: METHODS OF DISTRIBUTION

Method							Bonus
1 Equal Share	=	Pool / Number of participants	=	$10,000 / 100	=		$100
2 Equal %	=	Pool / Participating Payroll $	=	$10,000 / $100,000	=		10%
3 Equal cents/hour	=	Pool / Participating Hours	=	$10,000 / 10,000 hrs	=		10 cents per hour

worked. The team generates the gains, and all members of the team are rewarded the same dollars. Even today, the majority of employees prefer this alternative. Unfortunately, in the United States, the equal share alternative runs into problems if nonexempt employees (those covered by the Fair Labor Standards Act) are included in the plan. Basically, if nonexempt employees are plan participants, the equal share alternative will be illegal. The company will be found in violation of the Fair Labor Standards Act, commonly referred to as the wage and hour law. The gainsharing bonus payment is not the issue per se. The issue is that overtime premium will be improper, because an incorrect rate of pay will be used when multiplying the pay rate to the premium hours (pay rate x premium = premium pay). The rate of pay used in the payment of the overtime premium needs to include the value of any "incentives" earned for the period. A gainsharing bonus is considered to be an incentive under the Fair Labor Standards Act (FLSA). The Fair Labor Standards Act, Section 6457, reads in part:

> "**Compensation Status** — If the bonus payment is of the type required to be included in the employee's total compensation, it will cause an increase in his hourly rate of pay and a resulting increase in total compensation during work weeks in which overtime hours are worked. Whether a bonus must be taken into consideration when figuring an employee's overtime pay under the FLSA depends upon its purpose and its nature:
>
> (1) Bonuses which are designed to encourage increased efforts on the part of employees constitute earnings which must be included in overtime pay calculations."

For example, if employee John Doe worked eight hours over 40 in week one of a month, he would receive a premium of four hours (8 hours x ½ premium = 4 premium hours). Let's say that John is paid weekly at a base rate of $10 per hour. Therefore, he would receive $40 in premium pay (4 hours x $10 = $40). At the end of the month, all employees earn an equal share gainsharing bonus of $100. If the company's payroll records are audited, the wage and hour people will find that John was shorted on his overtime payment, $40 was not enough. Why? Because the rate of $10 per hour used in calculating the premium payment (4 x $10 = $40) was incorrect. The $10 rate did not include the hourly value of the $100 gainsharing "incentive" payment.

On the other hand, if the gainsharing bonus were based on a percentage of the individual employee's total earnings (both regular and premium earnings), the percentage award automatically would incorporate the value of the gainsharing incentive into the premium pay. If the gainsharing bonus calculated to be 10.5 percent, John Doe's bonus is as follows:

Percent of Payroll Bonus

Regular hours		40
Hours over 40		8
Premium	+	4
Total hours		52
Hour rate	x	$10.00
Weekly pay		$520.00
Gainsharing %	x	10.5%
Bonus		**$54.60**

Also, if the gainsharing bonus is paid on the basis of equal cents per hour, there will be no problem as long as the payout is based on hours paid (including the premium hours). If the gainsharing bonus were equal to $1 per hour, John Doe's bonus is calculated as follows:

Cents per hour Bonus

Regular hours		40
Hours over 40		8
Premium	+	4
Total hours		52
Gainsharing cents/hour	x	$1.00
Bonus		**$52.00**

Therefore, most organizations today distribute the gain based on either a percent of participating payroll or cents per participating hours. A design team also has to clearly define "participating" (hours or payroll). In other words, are hours paid for time not worked included as participating (hours or payroll)? If someone is on vacation for two weeks for the month, are the vacation earnings (hours) included as participating payroll (hours)? A pure pay-for-performance advocate likely would argue, "no."

Equal percent — The equal percentage method is perhaps the easiest method to administer. Those with higher earnings receive more. One can make a good argument that this approach makes sense because, at least in theory, higher paid people are paid more because they contribute more. Therefore, they should receive a larger gainsharing check. In some environments, this is a contentious issue since managers will receive a larger bonus. To soften the concern, some design teams decide, for the purpose of defining participating payroll, that exempt employees' participating payroll will be capped at some common dollar value reflecting the average compensation of nonexempt employees at the facility. Obviously, this will also cause the bonus percent to increase.

Equal cents per hour — The equal cents per hour approach is growing in popularity in organizations that have a large, nonexempt work force. In this case, people who are paid for more hours will get more. Therefore, those employees who work more overtime receive a larger bonus. This is always a sore point for employees that work in jobs that don't have the opportunity for overtime. However, employees who work more overtime also will receive more bonus dollars if the equal percentage method is used, but generally, the spread between the highest bonus dollars and the lowest is less when the equal cents per hour method is used.

The equal cents per hour method typically will provide managers the smallest bonus since managers aren't usually paid for overtime. Unfortunately, many managers are working longer hours than anyone else in the work force. To recognize this issue, some design teams decide to define the participating hours for exempt employees as the average hours worked for all nonexempt employees in the organization.

Split distribution — More recently, some design teams have decided to use a hybrid approach of distributing the gains to soften some concerns found in the equal percentage and equal cents per hour alternatives. I refer to the approach as a split distribution; the gains are being divided into two distribution pools. One distribution is for hourly and nonexempt personnel (those covered by the Fair Labor Standards Act). The second pool is for exempt personnel. Basically, the distribution pools are based on the ratios of eligible, nonexempt associates and eligible, exempt employees. Figure 43 provides an example.

FIGURE 43: SPLIT DISTRIBUTION

Allocation

Number of Employees	Number of Participants	% Of Participants		Total Pool	Split Pools
Exempt	20	20%	x	$10,000	$2,000
Nonexempt	80	80%	x	$10,000	$8,000
Total	100	100%			$10,000

Payout per Participant

Final Pools	Dollars	Participants		Bonus
Exempt	$2,000	20	=	$100
Nonexempt	$8,000	80	=	Cents per hour or % Bonus

In the split distribution example, the total employee pool is $10,000, and there are 100 participants. If the equal share method were used, $100 would be awarded per participant ($10,000/100 = $100). In this case, the exempt employees are paid in equal shares. In other words, the exempt employees receive $100, the facility average. The nonexempt employees either will be paid on the basis of equal percentage or equal cents per hour, depending on the design team's decision. The split distribution method is able to eliminate some of the controversy associated with the equal percentage alternative. Since managers typically have higher salaries than non-exempts, the equal percentage alternative generally will yield more dollars to managers. On the other hand, the split distribution alternative yields managers the average dollars paid to nonexempts.

10

Other Plan Policies

Many other plan design issues need to be resolved before the plan can be finalized. The following summary and comments cover a number of these issues.

Eligibility — Who and when? Are all employees included? How about employees eligible for other bonus payments? How about part-time, temporary and co-op employees? More and more employers are utilizing contract personnel. Should they be included? Are they part of the team? Do they influence the outcome? How about the top manager? Should he/she be eligible?

When should a new hire be included? Some may argue new hires don't initially contribute until they are fully trained. Someone else may argue, "A new hire should be eligible for gainsharing when he/she becomes eligible for the employee benefits plan." Is gainsharing a benefit plan, a pay-for-performance plan or a management system? How much turnover does the organization experience? Will gainsharing help as a recruitment tool? How about people who transfer to the site from another company facility? When would they be eligible?

My advice is to typically include everyone, unless there is a logical business reason to exclude some groups. In addition, include new hires on the first day they join the organization. After all, gainsharing brings everyone together as one team.

Termination policies — What happens when employees terminate employment? Do they get a portion of the gain? What happens if they are discharged? How about someone that is a reduction in force? Is a resignation handled differently than if someone retires? How would the quarterly or monthly payment be handled? Would they be eligible for the reserve? If so, should it be paid at year-end, or should they be cashed out when they leave the company? Maybe when the person left the company mid-year, the reserve was in a negative position, but at year-end, it's in a positive position. Should the person still get some of the reserve?

Gainsharing is not an entitlement. If people leave the organization during the performance period, they aren't eligible for that period's gain. After all, those remaining generally have to "dig in" when the organization is short-handed.

Plan Year — Most plans are based on a plan year. Every year, the plan is reviewed, and the baselines are adjusted. Most companies have the gainsharing plan year parallel the organization's accounting year but some organizations have found that it is better to have a different gainsharing plan than the accounting year.

My advice would be to have the plan year other than the calendar or business year. This will help assure that the plan gets the attention that it deserves. Remember, the first year can also be a partial year.

Communications — How will information be communicated? Who will be responsible? What's the frequency? I'm always surprised when managers and supervisors flinch at my suggestion of weekly gainsharing meetings. Some managers initially think that all that is necessary is to post the results, and the plan will run itself. Organizations that have the measurement data available should discuss performance weekly. What would happen if a football team only huddled once every four downs!

Remember the three C's of gainsharing: communications, communications and communications. Not cash, credit and currency.

Employee Involvement — Is there a current involvement system in place? If so, the current involvement system should be integrated into the gainsharing plan. If there is no formal involvement system, one needs to be developed when the plan is designed. The following issues need to be defined in a gainsharing plan:

- Number of involvement teams and makeup
- Review board
- Membership and term of office
- Frequency of meetings

- Roles and responsibilities
- Record keeping and communications requirements
- Spending limits.

To reiterate my earlier point, gainsharing is an employee involvement plan with teeth. If there is no involvement system, the plan will be short-lived.

11

The Design Team and Implementation Steps

Gainsharing is a tool to drive organizational change. As many businesses have learned, the best way to promote change is to get employees involved in the process. Therefore, after an organization has developed an understanding of the gainsharing philosophy, explored readiness and has determined to move forward, the next step is to engage the general employee population.

The first step is to form a design team or task force to develop many elements of the plan. The team consists of a cross-section of employees that mirrors the organization. Depending on the company's size, the group may consist of as few as four employees and as many as 30. Typically, the group consists of about 10 percent of the work force. Of course, in larger organizations, the percentage is less. The group typically meets once a week for approximately four hours. Usually, the design team phase takes about four months.

Why a Design Team?

The objective for having a design team is to develop employee ownership and identity to the gainsharing plan. Basically, the organization will have a group of homegrown gainsharing disciples. The design team is given a set of top-management-approved parameters laying the foundation for the team's focus. As the team wrestles with the issues, members develop identity and ownership. They build the plan and help ensure that it will work once implemented. If people build their own home, they have a high level of ownership in the project. Moreover, they take especially good care of it once it is built.

Also, many of the gainsharing plan's policies are related to social issues, such as who's eligible and when. In some cases, there is no one clear answer. It is best to get employees involved. If the plan is developed by top managers or human resources, whose plan is it?

Should an outside consultant be used? The right consultant can be very helpful in the process, but his/her job should not be to serve as the developer of the plan. A consultant can help provide insight to many plan alternatives, assure that the overall design is appropriate and help the organization avoid any pitfalls. Gainsharing is a nontraditional approach and it is very easy to slip back into traditional ways of thinking. However, the consulting role should be to facilitate and advise and not to provide a turnkey plan.

Design Team's Role

The design team needs to have an understanding of the basic principles and philosophy of gainsharing. Team members will be the authors of the plan; therefore, they will develop a strong understanding for its measures and policies. The team typically has special bulletin boards to post meeting minutes, Q&A's and other information on plan developments. However, its role is not to serve as representatives for other groups or departments. (See Sidebar: A Word of Caution on page 111.) In other words, the team does not solicit views and opinions from other employees in order to represent these views in the development process. The design team is given management-approved guidelines for areas to be explored and resolved. Rather than serving as representatives, the team operates more like a jury; all decisions are made by consensus. The group talks through the issues and evaluates the pros and cons. Eventually the design team makes a consensus decision on what it thinks is appropriate. Its role is not to make decisions based upon other employees' requests.

Since the team will be making decisions based on the consensus decision-making model, design team meetings may, on occasion, become contentious. However, because the quality of decision-making is solid, all members eventually should be strongly supportive of the final decisions. Again, the team operates like a jury, not as politicians.

When the team has completed the plan, it formally presents the plan to top management for final approval. Once approved, the group presents the plan to the total work force. Typically, teams use a variety of innovative techniques to promote and kick off the plan. The team also needs to develop an ongoing communications system and methods for orienting new employees. Over the long term, the team should be involved in monitoring the plan against its initial plan objectives and should meet formally at least once per year to review plan modifications. The design team is a crucial part of the change process; without it, the change likely will not occur.

Who's on the Team?

The design team should have employees from all departments and levels. If 10 percent of the work force is in the lab, then 10 percent of the design team should be from the lab. If 40 percent of the work force is salaried, then about 40 percent of employees on the team should be salaried. Typically, team members are selected from a group of volunteers after the total work force has been oriented to the gainsharing concept and the team's role. The steering committee that explored the gainsharing initiative selects design team members. If the facility is a union site, union officials should participate in the steering committee.

Typically, the top manager and union head official are not on the team in order to avoid their domination of the group. However, it depends on the culture and the individuals involved. Some key managers should participate on the team. It is critical that a key accounting or financial professional is involved. His/her participation helps the team have an understanding of the numbers and develops creditability and trust in the person who eventually may be responsible for generating gainsharing reports. Gainsharing is a wonderful opportunity for the accountant/financial people to be more involved in their role as educators. Very often, someone from human resources is on the team. A human resources person often facilitates the process and handles the administrative details. It also is good to have managers, engineers or other professionals involved that are very familiar with operational measures. Remember to have first-line supervisor representation on the team. In the final analysis, first-line supervisors will be key to the plan's success.

The hourly members of the group should be the facility's opinion leaders. The key is that the person is respected by peers and has the ability to work with other team members. It's best to have someone who could be a potential barrier to the plan's success involved up front rather than having that person "throw stones" once the plan has been implemented. The following is a list of typical criteria for the selection of the design team members:

> **Criteria For Choosing A Design Team Member**
> - Is respected by peers
> - Is an opinion leader, someone who feels free to speak up
> - Is a good listener, open and flexible to others' opinions
> - Is a team player
> - Has knowledge of the operations and business.

Parameters for Team's Decision-making

What should the design team address, all of the elements of the plan or a more limited list of items? Like so many things in gainsharing, it depends on the organization. Basically, gainsharing components can be divided between policy/social and technical/calculation issues. (See Figure 44 on page 110.) Of course, some issues are both technical and social.

One approach is to have the design team focus on the social issues, and have the management steering team focus on the technical issues. Another approach is to have the design team focus on all of the issues, or to perhaps divide the design team into subgroups to address specific issues (the calculation, policies, involvement system). The management steering team and design team approach is very common. However, all of these approaches typically work well as long as the process is properly managed.

If the organization uses the dual committee approach, typically the management staff steering team focuses on the technical components (measures, sharing baselines, gates, etc.) and the design team focuses on the policy and communications issues. The technical issues involve pouring over detailed numbers, developing formulas, gathering additional data, reviewing the numbers again, etc. Often, if the full design team works on this activity, the process can become very dry for many team members, and they may become bogged down. The process has a tendency to take a few months longer. On the other hand, managers are familiar with dealing with measurement data. In addition, they are well-equipped at identifying the "whys" behind some of the monthly swings in the data. Managers are more familiar with the potential shortcomings of a specific measure. The biggest advantage of the dual committee approach is that managers are involved in the process and develop more commitment and ownership of the plan. It's important for managers to see gainsharing as everyone's plan, not just the employees' plan. Whatever is measured should be the tools that management uses to drive the business. In terms of the calculation, the design team's role would be to review measures in order to develop a thorough understanding, determine fairness and fine-tune as necessary.

Implementation Steps

A significant amount of organizational commitment is necessary to install a

FIGURE 44: PLAN COMPONENTS

Policy/Social

Purpose and Goals
Identity statement
Eligibility (who, when)
   Who (hourly, management, temporary, part-time, contract)
   When (new hires, rehires, transfers, layoffs, leaves of absence)
Payment policies
   Method of distribution
   Minimum payment
   Separate check, normal payroll check
Reserve
   Plan year
   Eligibility
   Method of Distribution
Involvement Structure
   Determine relationship to current involvement activities
   Team structure

Member selection
Term of office
Members' roles
Spending limits
Recording keeping
Frequency of meetings
Communications
   Communications team
   Postings
   Bulletin Boards
   Meetings
   Newsletter
Design Team
   Initial role
   Long-term role
   Membership replacement
Auditing provisions
Plan Name

Technical/Calculation

Measurements
Definition of the group(s)
Values for calculating gains
Sharing Percent
Deficit Reserve

Gates
Payout frequency
Baselines
Method of changing baseline

---

gainsharing plan. The total work force needs to be educated on gainsharing and employee involvement concepts. The use of a design team will mean that a number of employees will be involved in about 12 meetings, four hours each, over a course of three to four months. Many team members may need to be replaced on the job while they attend team meetings. In a multishift operation, all shifts should be represented on the design team. Shift schedules need to be accommodated. Someone in the organization will have to gather data, so a cal-

A Word of Caution

Concerning the National Labor Relations Act's definition of a "labor organization" and the possibility of management's "illegal domination" of such a group organization, the design team's role is not to serve as representatives for other employees. Nor is its role to work in a negotiating process with management.

The reader may be familiar with the well-publicized 1992 National Labor Relations Board (NLRB) decision commonly referred to as the Electromation case. Basically, the case involved employee "action committees" which were set up by Electromation Inc. at its Elkhart, Ind., plant. The nonunion company established five action committees in 1989 after receiving a petition signed by 68 workers opposing certain compensation changes that had been unilaterally implemented by management.

The action committees were established to address five issues of employee dissatisfaction: absenteeism/infractions, no smoking policy, communication network, pay progression and an attendance bonus program. The committees were given the role of soliciting the views of other employees on these subjects. The committees met with management to discuss alternative approaches to resolve these problems, and in turn, the committees followed up with employees regarding their progress. One month after establishing the committees, a union demanded recognition as the exclusive bargaining agent. According to a judge's finding, there was no evidence that the company knew of the union's organizing drive before this time. However, the NLRB held that the electronics company imposed on its employees its own labor organization and its own unilateral form of bargaining. The board ordered Electromation to "immediately disestablish" the action committees and stop giving assistance or other support to the committees.

Three key points relate to the 1992 Electromation case and the formation of a design team. First, the company needs to ensure that the design team does not operate in a representational capacity. The team needs to avoid acting as a "go-between" for management and other employees. Its role is not to serve as a representative for co-workers. Second, the design team process should not be handled as a negotiation. The purpose of the design team is to make recommendations on various plan elements and, in turn, submit the recommended plan for final management approval. Third, and perhaps most important, an environment in which employees are circulating petitions or otherwise strongly express their dissatisfaction with the company is no place to initiate gainsharing. The organization truly is not ready.

culation can be developed. Meeting minutes and a plan document must be prepared. Supervisors and managers need to be trained in their role of managing in a gainsharing environment. Employee involvement teams will need to be trained. The total work force needs to be trained in the plan and how it impacts results. The process generally takes six months or more. More importantly, once a plan is installed, it doesn't run itself. It needs to be managed.

Figure 45 shows the typical flow of the implementation process.

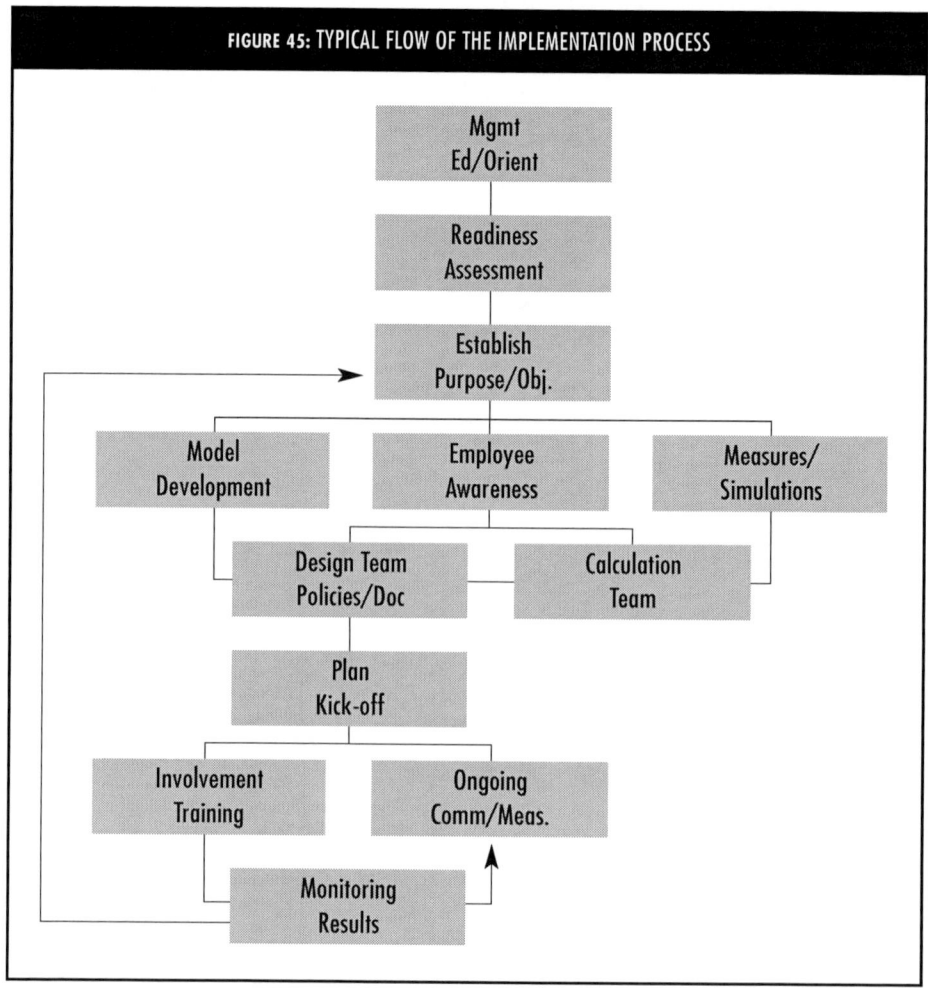

Step 1: Education/Orientation of Management Staff

The objective of this first phase is to develop a common understanding among management of the basics of the gainsharing philosophy and its key principles. It is critical that the entire management team recognizes the level of ongoing commitment required for the plan's success. It's best that there is a consensus among management team members to move forward with gainsharing. The exploration process is similar to approaches used to study other improvement initiatives: use of outside consultants, attending seminars, readings and visits to other sites with gainsharing plans. Some managers have been exploring gainsharing for years; for others, the concept is relatively new.

Readiness Assessment Checklist

Readiness needs to be thoroughly explored. If an organization is not fully prepared, has a false start or if the plan fails, organizational trust will be damaged. The following checklist offers some key factors to consider when exploring readiness:

- Does top management really believe in people?
- Does management think it's fair to share?
- Are the key managers competent in their area of expertise?
- Will corporate be supportive?
- Is the organization capable of sticking with gainsharing over the long haul? Does the organization have a history of implementing improvement initiatives in a half-hearted manner?
- What's the likelihood that the organization's top manager will be at the same site during the next two years?
- Does the management team effectively work together?
- What is the level of organizational trust? Is it going down or has the organization turned the corner?
- Are there other major initiatives that the organization is undertaking that will channel resources away from the gainsharing endeavor?
- Does the work environment require collaboration between individuals and groups?
- Does the organization currently have an individual incentive plan in place? If so, how will it be eliminated?
- Do employees work an excessive amount of overtime? Will workers see gainsharing as a threat to future overtime opportunities?
- If the facility is unionized, is there a cooperative working relationship between union and management officials?
- Have prior gainsharing or bonus initiatives been attempted and failed? If so, why?

- Will the first-line supervisors be receptive to employees becoming more involved?
- Does the organization constructively address performance problems?
- How open is communication? Does the company openly share financial and other performance information?
- Are employees currently threatened by the potential of layoffs or job losses?
- What is the status of the business cycle? Is business activity declining, stable or in an upward swing?
- Is there a strong person in the organization that can serve as a cheerleader for gainsharing?
- Most important: Is the organization willing to change?

Step 2: Purpose and Goals

Assuming that the management staff is prepared to move forward, the next step is to clearly define the purpose for installing a gainsharing plan and determine the outcomes the organization wants to achieve. The plan's purpose lays the foundation for the gainsharing design.

Step 3: Employee Awareness

The objective of the awareness phase is to provide everyone in the organization an understanding of the gainsharing concept. Organizationwide commitment for gainsharing and the recognition for the need for change must be addressed. This typically is done through facilitywide meetings/education sessions. At this point, the organization should solicit feedback from everyone regarding his/her desire for moving forward with gainsharing. Why or why not? An organizationwide survey is an effective tool to solicit feedback.

Traditional gainsharing plans called for an employee vote once the plan was fully completed. I prefer that employees' input be solicited well before the plan is developed in order to secure organizationwide commitment for proceeding. Approximately 90 percent of the work force should agree to proceed. Why would employees say, "No?" In some organizations, trust levels are so low that gainsharing may never work. Also, if an organization is very weak and has a number of nonperformers, people may view gainsharing as a threat. Gainsharing is not a cure-all. If employees are not in favor of installing a plan, management needs to address the restrainers and move forward at another time.

Some of the best successes stories are found at facilities that have deferred gainsharing until the deeper-seated problems were fully addressed. A recent example of a plant in central Indiana reinforces this point.

The Indiana facility is a relatively mature plant with approximately 85 employees. Over the years, a very autocratic plant manager ruled the facility. When a new plant manager arrived with a more open and participative style, there were many scars to mend. In fact, many years prior, the plant had abandoned a poorly managed bonus system. The new plant manager was eager to install a gainsharing plan, but the results of a readiness survey clearly indicated that a number of trust and communications issues needed to be addressed before the facility proceeded with gainsharing. After about one year, as issues were addressed, many of the less-vocal employees expressed an interest in re-exploring gainsharing. After a six-month design period, the plan was kicked off. Gains were generated for the first three payout periods, and after six months, the management team felt that the plant had finally turned the corner.

Step 4: Model Development, Measures and Simulations

This phase depends on the approach the organization plans to take with the design team. Some conservative businesses prefer to explore measures and potential calculation models before proceeding to Step 3, employee awareness. This is particularly true for an organization piloting gainsharing in a larger multi-facility company. Top management may want to know, "How much money is gainsharing going to make, and how much is it going to cost?" In a more conservative organization, a fair amount of upfront work may be done before the design team is formed. On the other hand, the design team or the dual steering/design team may develop the calculation component. Regardless, at this point, the organization needs to apply its calculation philosophy: physical/control orientation or financial/common-fate orientation.

Step 5: Design Team Formal Plan Development Phase

During this phase, the design team is selected and trained in its role, gainsharing components, consensus decision-making and meeting effectiveness. The team typically selects a chairperson, vice chairperson and recorder. Generally it's best that the chairperson is not a manager. There is a need for nonmanagement people to be highly involved.

Depending on the organization's implementation approach, the team may form subgroups. A communications team is a popular design team subcommittee. The product of the design group's effort will be a detailed gainsharing plan document. Toward the end of the process, the team conducts an organization-wide contest to name the plan. The contest aids in the group's communication and promotional activities. The team also should identify and address barriers for the plan's success.

At the end of the development phase, the design team will present the plan to top management. At least one or two key managers should participate on the team to avoid any last-minute management surprises.

Step 6: Plan Kickoff

The design team launches the plan through organizationwide communication/education sessions. Generally, all design team members participate in the kick-off presentation. For some, this is a major demonstration of their commitment since they are highly uncomfortable in front of a large group. For many members, serving on the design team is a personal/professional development experience.

Some design teams are very creative in their plan launch activities. Teams use contests, skits, cookouts, raffles and other innovative tools to help promote the kickoff. All employees are given a copy of the plan document. A word of caution: the kickoff meeting is what it is, a kickoff. The team now has to play the game. Just because the full plan has been communicated doesn't mean that employees understand it. Much more follow-up education is required. Organizations that follow up with immediate training get off to a much better start than those who take shortcuts.

Step 7: Implementation/Training

Involvement Training — Gainsharing promotes change. If it is implemented properly, employees become more focused, and as they become more focused, problems will surface. If supervisors are not prepared, or if there are no means of presenting solutions to these problems, the plan will eventually fail.

Supervisors need to be trained in their changing roles in a gainsharing environment. Training topics should include change management, employee involvement and effective communications.

After kickoff, employee involvement teams are formed. The team members need to be trained in the involvement system being utilized. Training should at least cover the involvement system, record keeping, establishing team norms, conducting meetings and providing feedback. Also, there is an ongoing need for the teams to be supported and mentored.

General employee training and communication — It's critical that shortly after kickoff, all employees go through more specific plan training, particularly in terms of the measurement and involvement systems. People need to recognize that if they do their jobs exactly as they have in the past, there will be no gain; dollars will not fall from the sky.

In addition, managers and supervisors need to have at least monthly meetings to discuss results, recognize good performance, review future work plans and point out potential problems. The objective is to heighten the level of awareness. Initially, gains are generated simply because the level of employee awareness has been elevated. If there is little communication, awareness will not be advanced. The meetings shouldn't be used as a means of browbeating employees. I recall one plant manager using this approach, and the facility took two steps backward. Fortunately, the plant manager was eventually replaced.

Plan Coordinator — A point person is needed once the plan is kicked off to coordinate plan activities. This typically can be done in smaller facilities without adding to staff. Larger facilities of perhaps 200 or more employees should have a full- or part-time coordinator. Spartan Light Metals Products, a gainsharing company, took an innovative approach to address the issue. The Spartan design team felt it was critical that the plan have a full-time coordinator. The cost of the person was split 50/50 between the employee and company's share of the gain. In addition, the design team was involved in selecting the coordinator.

When the coordinator's role is handled without adding resources, often someone in human resources serves in the position. Other facilities have established a gainsharing administration team. The team may consist of employees from human resources, accounting and a customer service representative. Some of the best coordinators have come from the hourly ranks. People often surface and shine from their involvement on the design team. Regardless, there is a need for a cheerleader.

Step 8: Monitoring Phase

After implementation, the plan needs to be monitored. The design team initially gets back together every quarter or semiannually to evaluate how the plan is performing. The full team also meets at the end of the year to review and make necessary adjustments. In addition to changes in the baseline, new measures may be added, and other measures may be modified or discontinued.

I encourage organizations to conduct a follow-up monitoring survey near the end of the first plan year. The survey may be done earlier, especially if there are problems. The survey should solicit employee opinions regarding the gainsharing plan's performance against the initial plan purpose and objectives. Also, feedback should be collected regarding management's support of the plan, the effectiveness of the involvement system and perceptions regarding the bonus calculation.

Figure 46 on pages 119 and 120 is a timeline used by a 25-employee design team in a facility of 1,600-plus employees.

FIGURE 46: IMPLEMENTATION PLAN TIMELINE

What	Who	When
Management team gainsharing orientation	Mgmt team, consultant	4/1
Management readiness assessment	Mgmt team, consultant	5/15
Management development of plan purpose	Mgmt team, consultant	5/20
Management team identifies boundaries for gainsharing	Mgmt team, consultant	6/1
Management team explores possible measures	Mgmt team, consultant	7/1
All-employee awareness sessions and survey	Consultant	7/15
Design team formation	Mgmt team	8/1
• Design team training	Consultant	8/17
Complete plan document	Design team (D.T.) consultant	
• Design team's mission statement		8/18
• Purpose and goals		8/18
• Eligibility		9/1
• Termination policies		9/15
• Reserve eligibility		9/15
• Method of distribution		9/22
• Measurement review and refinement		10/27
• Frequency of payout		10/27
• Minimum payout		11/3
• Plan name		11/3
• Employee and management plan responsibilities		11/24
• Identity statement		11/24
• Involvement system		
- Structure of teams		11/17
- Review board		11/17
- Term of office		11/17
- Spending level		11/17
• Communication system		11/24

FIGURE 46: IMPLEMENTATION PLAN TIMELINE (CONTINUED)

Corporate approval	D.T.	12/8
Plantwide promotional activities	D.T.	
• Distribution of plan document to all employees		12/11
• Contests, newsletter, mailer		12/11
• One-on-one-contacts		12/12
Plant-wide kick-off communications	D.T.	
• Shift meetings to present plan details		12/16
• Luncheon, raffle, T-shirts		12/16
Manager/supv training	Consultant	12/18
• Role development and expectations for supvs.		
Plan Becomes Effective		**1/1**
Involvement team selected	D.T.	1/3
Performance postings	D.T., plan coordinator	1/6
• (Some daily, weekly, monthly)		
Involvement Team activities		
• Team training	Consultant	1/6
Initial employee training	D.T., consultant	1/7
• Small group sessions		
First team meeting	Team(s), plan adm.	1/13
First review board meeting	Team(s), review board	2/7
Department shift communication meetings on results	D.T., supervisor	2/10
Follow-up employee training	D.T, plan adm.	2/15
• Plan quiz		
• Brainstorming		
Monitoring survey	D.T., consultant	7/1
Preparation for 2nd plan year	Design team	11/1
Communication of plan changes as appropriate	Design team	12/1

12

The Employee Involvement System

I often use an analogy of a freight train when discussing gainsharing. The cars on the train are the measures. Some cars may be bigger than others, and therefore, they carry a greater share of the load, just as some measures in a gainsharing plan carry more weight for the organization's future success. If the train never gets started and sits at the station, it will never get to its destination. The same is true for gainsharing; if the organization doesn't change, and if people don't do things differently, there will be no gain.

Like a train that gets off to a slow start and gradually picks up momentum as it moves on, many gainsharing plans initially have small gains. However, as the small gains are shared, more and more people take notice and start to do work differently. The ultimate success of the train reaching its final destination is dependent on the power and efficiency of its engine. Gainsharing's engine is employee involvement. Without a structured system of employee involvement, gainsharing will fall far short of its potential destination.

There are many systems of employee involvement ranging from basic communications meetings, taskforces, idea teams, problem-solving teams and self-directed work teams. The type of involvement system used in a gainsharing plan depends on the organizational culture, style of management and the prior level of involvement activities. There are many alternative involvement systems. However, one of the most common approaches found in gainsharing is a team-based idea (suggestion) system. Basically, employee involvement teams are formed to solicit and review suggestions from other members of the work force. The groups are permanent and meet on a regular basis to discuss ideas and suggestions. They have limited spending authority to approve and implement suggestions. Suggestions that are approved by a team, but are beyond its spending authority, are advanced to a higher level in the organization for final approval. Unlike a traditional suggestion system, a team-based system does not provide individual monetary rewards.

Involvement Teams — The team structure varies from one gainsharing plan to the next in order to best fit each organization's needs. Often, each department has a team. In a shift operation, there may be one team per shift and other teams for support departments. In other cases, teams may be cross-functional groups. One cross-function team is formed for each plan measure. Regardless of the structure, the teams consist of about four to six employees. Members typically are made up of hourly, professional and supervisory employees. In some cases, a manager may be a member. In other cases, managers may serve as a team mentor. Members generally serve a term of 12 to 18 months.

Involvement team members are responsible for soliciting performance improvement suggestions and developing a full understanding of each suggestion. In turn, the team members investigate suggestions by collaborating with other employees including supervisors, engineers and other support personnel. Those offering suggestions sometimes are involved in the process. The full team meets at least once a month to discuss ideas and make decisions either to approve, further investigate or decline ideas. Groups generally are given from $500 to $1,000 spending authority to implement an idea. However, the team members must reach a consensus before approval. Also, the team is responsible for follow-up to assure that ideas are implemented. At the end of each team meeting, members are given assignments to give feedback to each suggester and to further investigate open ideas.

The Review Board — Ideas approved by the involvement team that exceed its spending level are forwarded to the review board. This group generally consists of the captains of each involvement team and top site officials. Often, the top manager, controller and human resources manager participate on the board. It's best that there are at least as many nonmanagement members as management members on the review board. Each involvement team makes a report on its activities and presents larger spending ideas. The review board also has the role of overseeing the gainsharing plan.

During the monthly review board meeting, the organization's performance is reviewed, and bonus results are announced. Business trends and operating problems also are discussed to direct the teams to problem areas where idea generation can be focused. Task forces may be formed, if needed. Figure 47 on page 124 is an example of the idea flow.

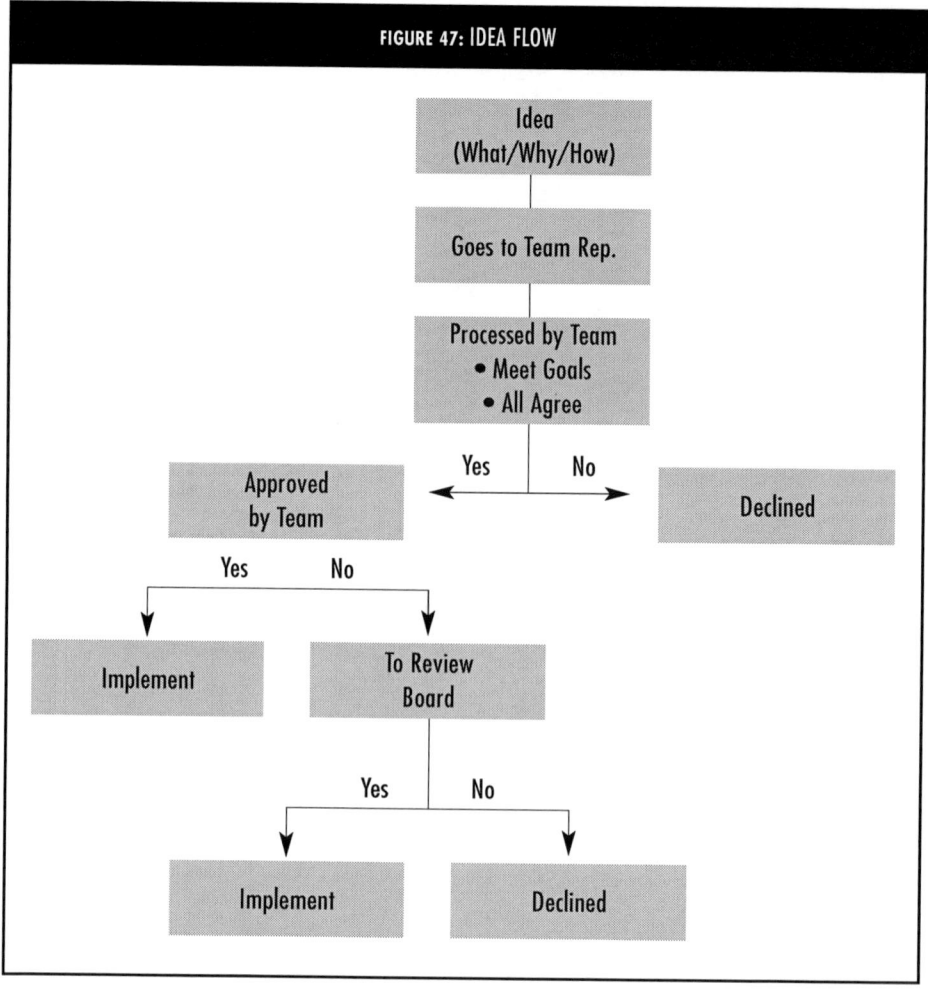

FIGURE 47: IDEA FLOW

A critical part of the involvement system is the careful consideration of all ideas and the requirement of prompt feedback to the submitter. Improvements are made one step at a time through many small ideas. Companies have been known to receive employee suggestions that have cost more than $500,000 in capital, and have returned enormous gains. However, most suggestions cost very little. I recall a plastics extrusion plant that experienced long delays in product changeovers when a particular compound was manufactured. The problem was that the extruder screw would heat up when the compound was run. When it was necessary to clean out the extruder, the residue was very difficult to remove. An engineer was in the process of designing an expensive cooling jacket that would prevent the residue from sticking to the inside of the extruder. As the engineer and operators discussed the problem, one operator asked, "What would happen if we put a bag of ice through the machine on the final run?" After some discussion, the engineer agreed that the ice would have no adverse impact on the equipment. The operator drove to the nearest convenience store and returned with the bag of ice. They tried the experiment. The residual material popped out as clean as a whistle.

The involvement structure not only encourages participation but also provides a means of enhancing two-way communications regarding plan goals. Recognition in a variety of ways is encouraged and promoted. However, the idea system is intended to be more than a performance improvement and communication tool. A broader objective is developing organizational trust. The idea system helps foster respect. In other words, if employees feel their ideas are listened to, are given prompt feedback and see their ideas promptly implemented, they will feel that they are respected. Obviously, everyone wants to be respected. As people feel more respected, their trust in the organization begins to grow and develop.

As discussed earlier, the foundation for today's gainsharing plans came from Joe Scanlon in the 1930s. When Scanlon's plan was initially implemented, it was a system of getting people more involved through their ideas and suggestions. When the plan was first implemented, there were no monetary rewards or bonus system. However, a few years later, Scanlon devised an organizationwide bonus formula. As performance improved through employee efforts and suggestions, the gains were shared with everyone on a monthly basis. Basically the Scanlon philosophy says, "As we work together to improve the operations, everyone shares in the financial benefits."

13

End Results

The results of a successful gainsharing plan can be thought of in both technical (business) and social outcomes. One can research many articles on gainsharing success stories and impressive research studies. One of the most comprehensive studies to date was sponsored by WorldatWork (formerly the American Compensation Association) in conjunction with GTE, Maritz Inc., Monsanto Co., Motorola SPS and Travelers. The group was known as the Consortiums for Alternative Reward Strategies Research (CARS). In 1992, a CARS study titled "Capitalizing on Human Assets" focused on rewards plans for primarily nonmanagement employees designed to improve organizational performance. The study identified 2,200 organizations with performance-based reward plans. After a stringent screening process, 432 plans were examined in depth. The following is a summary of some of the key findings.

- Performance rewards plans are viewed by their organizations as business strategies. The objective is to develop human assets as opposed to traditional compensation programs, which tend to focus on attracting and retaining employees.
- Performance rewards plans operate effectively in a variety of environments: service, manufacturing, union and nonunion.
- Plans report better results when employees are more involved in their design and implementation.
- Operational plans typically show a 3-to-1 return ratio of total gain to payout.
- Operational plans report better performance improvement and greater satisfaction with results than plans using only bottom-line financial measures.
- More organizations in the study installed performance-reward plans to lead rather than support cultural change.

- While top-management support is critical to the success of the plan, support from middle managers, and especially first-line supervisors, has a major impact on the results.

My personal experience in a large and varied group of organizations confirms each of these findings. The study's results ring true for large as well as small organizations, private versus publicly held companies, union versus nonunion environments. The findings are as true today as in 1992. In fact, I'm surprised that more organizations have not installed plans.

A follow-up study of CARS conducted in 1997 took a more microapproach. Eleven plants were studied in detail including employee surveys focus groups and manager interviews. The study gauged the overall effectiveness of each plan. The study confirmed that the plan's effectiveness is strongly influenced by the strength of the local management's support for it. It gets back to commitment. In other words, the more managers put into the plan, the more they will get out of it. The study findings reinforce the point that employees need to understand the plan and have the *ability to influence the measures*. Also, the study stresses the importance of communication; *the more frequently people think about the plan, the greater the effectiveness.*

Actual Results

There are many examples of positive results, but the following three can give the reader a sense of what can be accomplished through a successful plan. The first example is a relatively new chemical plant in Kentucky. The gainsharing plan was installed five years after the startup of the operations. The plant had approximately 60 employees. Everyone in the operation was a participant in the plan. Similar to other gainsharing facilities, a team-based suggestion system was used to support employee involvement. Figure 48 shows the initial plan year results.

The measurement system primarily focused on: productivity, quality, returns and spending. Returns were based on product that customers

FIGURE 48: POSITIVE RESULTS FROM GAINSHARING

Annualized Gain	$616,000
Annualized dollars paid	$186,000
Cents per hour payout	$1.78
Estimated % payout per employee	11.5%
Ratio: Gain to payout	3.3 to 1

returned due to employee errors. The returns measure also served as a gatekeeper measure for productivity. In other words, gains from productivity first had to pass through a "return gate" before sharing could occur.

As Figure 49 shows, the plan was installed in July. The first plan year gains were primarily driven by improvements in productivity. Productivity was measured on the basis of total adjusted good pounds produced per hour worked. Work hours included salaried and wage employees hours worked. The output measure, "adjusted good pounds," was as follows:

$$\begin{array}{r} \text{Gross pounds} \\ \text{Less off-spec pounds} \\ \underline{\text{Less 3 time return pounds}} \\ \text{Adjusted good pounds} \end{array}$$

Returned pounds were weighted three times in order to emphasize the importance of serving the customer.

In this example, the first year results were better than the norm. The facility did an especially good job with the post-kickoff training and weekly communications. In this case, the baseline moved up in the second plan year as productivity continued to improve.

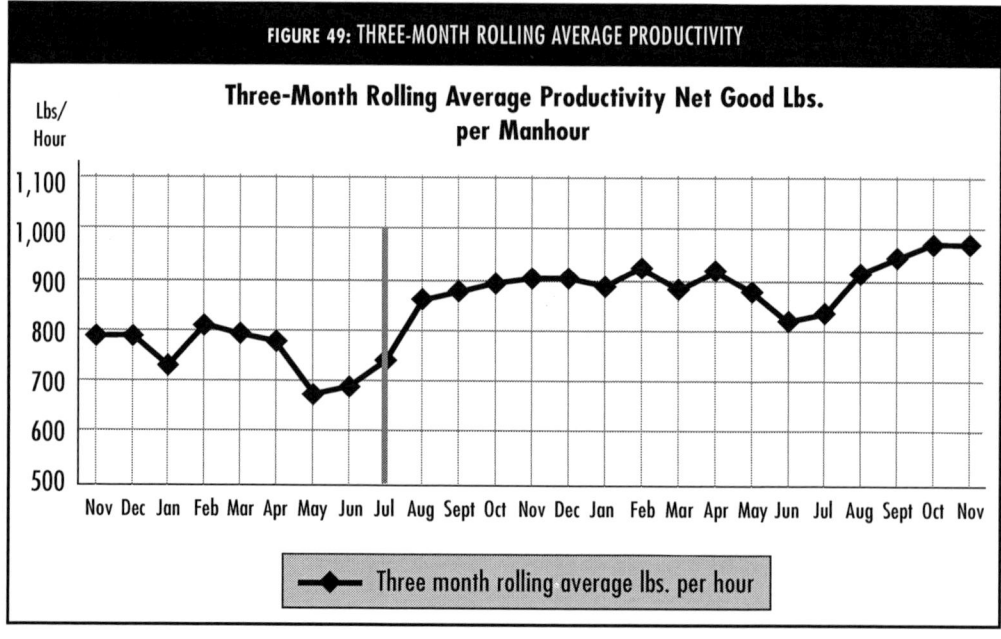

FIGURE 49: THREE-MONTH ROLLING AVERAGE PRODUCTIVITY

A second example is for a molded goods operations in Georgia employing 75 people. Before gainsharing, the facility experienced a relatively high degree of employee turnover because of industrial development in the community. Figure 50 provides a summary of the first plan year results.

In this example, the company shared 50 percent of the gain. Quality was measured in terms of three sub-measures: returns, process scrap and extrusion scrap. Scrap was counted separately for the extrusion operations and the downstream processes. The values used in the quality measures were as follows:

FIGURE 50: MOLDING OPERATIONS, FIRST-YEAR PLAN RESULTS

Measures Improvement	Baseline Quality	First-Year Results	%
• Returns	0.83%	0.49%	41.60%
• Process Scrap	0.72%	0.05%	25.50%
• Extrusion Scrap	16.80%	15.00%	10.50%
Productivity	66.2	64.9	-1.95%
Average Bonus	6%		

Type of Scrap	Value per pound
Returns	$1.00
Process Scrap	$0.50
Extrusion Scrap	$0.25

Of the three quality measures, returns improved by 41 percent, process scrap by 25 percent and extrusion scrap by 10 percent. The results clearly indicate that the employee focus and the corresponding improvements paralleled the importance (values) of each of the quality measures. Today, the operation's quality is very good, and the focus has turned to productivity (while maintaining quality). In addition, the facility is considering a spending measure.

The final example is in a 95-employee metal extrusion operation in Missouri. The operation is in a depressed community. The level of unemployment and poverty in the county is one of the highest in the state. Education levels are relatively low, and the company typically experiences a high degree of turnover. Many workers are the sole family provider. When I first visited the organization, I could sense the lack of confidence. The sense of pride and ownership was relatively low. Also, scrap levels were much higher than industry standards.

When the plan was developed, the design team specified that the plan's primary purpose was "to improve teamwork, cooperation and communications at all levels of the organization." The design team decided to name the plan "WOW," which stood for "Work On Winning." The measurement system was operational: direct employee productivity, support employee productivity, returns, process scrap and press scrap.

Because of cultural considerations, employee involvement was very basic. The initial focus was on communications and awareness. Each department had a 10- to 15-minute weekly meeting in which the supervisor reviewed the prior week and month-to-date performance figures. Also, a brief brainstorming session was conducted at the end of each meeting to identify ideas for improvement. Ideas would be written on a flip chart for follow-up in subsequent meetings. The weekly meetings were referred to as "WOW meetings." The first year plan results are in Figure 51.

FIGURE 51: METAL EXTRUSION OPERATION FIRST-YEAR PLAN RESULTS

	% Improvement
Direct Productivity	11%
Indirect Productivity	5%
Returns	40%
Process Scrap	-5%
Press scrap	16%
Average Bonus	**7%**

The results generated a handsome improvement for the company and an average employee bonus of 7 percent, including approximately $1,200 per employee in the year-end reserve account. Notably, the performance in process scrap was worse in the initial year. On the other hand, return scrap improved by 40 percent. Obviously, employees were catching defects before parts were shipped to the customer. In the second plan year, more emphasis was put on press scrap. The feeling was that scrap had to be caught earlier in the production process (at the press) in order to drive down process scrap and plant cost. In addition, in the second plan year, the plant advanced the level of involvement to a team-based suggestion system.

A shift in employee attitudes was another very important outcome. Frequent visitors to the plant noted a marked change in attitudes. "Employees felt more like winners." They took more pride in their jobs. The social results of the WOW plan are apparent from the findings in a comparison of pre- and post-gainsharing surveys with six common questions. The results are in Figure 52.

The perceptions regarding information sharing increased by 16 percent and employees' understanding of the plant's goals increased by 14 percent. The survey findings regarding communications and identity are very similar to those found in other organizations

FIGURE 52: SURVEY COMPARISON ONE YEAR AFTER IMPLEMENTATION

SCALE

1	2	3	4	5
Strongly Disagree	Disagree	Neither Agree nor Disagree	Agree	Strongly Agree

	Pre-Gainsharing	Post-Gainsharing	% Change
Teamwork & Cooperation			
People from different departments cooperate with each other well.	2.74	2.90	5.5%
Communications			
Communications between my supervisor and myself are good.	3.72	4.17	10.8%
I receive enough information for me to do my job well.	3.33	3.99	16.5%
Communications between departments are good.	2.74	2.96	7.4%
Trust			
I trust plant management here.	3.13	3.57	12.3%
Identity & Ownership			
I understand the plant's overall goals and objectives.	3.59	4.16	13.7%

after their first year of gainsharing. Generally, employee focus and awareness improved, leading to higher feelings about communication and identity. Also, trust improved by 12 percent. Trust typically does not increase this much in the first year; it's a long-term process. Questions related to relationships between departments improved, but not as significantly. Improvements related to cooperation and communications between departments take more time and require more change.

A Process to Develop Human Assets

Gainsharing is a very common-sense system. However, sadly, some organizations embark on installing a plan without an adequate understanding of and respect for the concept. A key theme is that gainsharing is a powerful tool to promote organizational change. It is a system that engages the total work force and one that provides a common focus. Gainsharing is more of a process to develop human assets, rather than strictly a compensation program.

The following are some of the critical factors for success which have been presented:

- Each plan must be specifically designed to fit the unique location and operation. There is no one perfect plan or formula.
- Employees must be involved in the process of designing and installing a gainsharing plan. Identity to the plan must be developed.
- The bonus formula drives the specific behavior that the organization desires to achieve, whether it is productivity, quality, cost or other organizational goals. Employees must perceive the linkage between pay and performance.
- The bonus calculation must be fair to the company, as well as employees. It must not be overly complex, but enough so that it accurately reflects business needs.
- Progress must be closely monitored to ensure the plan's viability. Changes need to be made that reflect the business, as well as employee perceptions of fairness.
- Employee involvement is a critical element of a gainsharing plan. Higher levels of involvement lead to new behaviors and improved organizational performance. It is a process of evolution, changing as the organization and its human resources develop.
- Training is critical. A solid foundation of management, supervisory and employee training enhances the chance of success.
- The top manager needs to be a champion of gainsharing and believer in his people. Also, assigning a coordinator in a supporting role is very important to guarantee continuing success.

Most importantly, to be effective, any plan requires an ongoing process of education and communications. Management commitment needs to exist to ensure success and demonstrate the willingness to change. The organization must believe in its people and fully recognize the contributions that they can make. Gainsharing is a powerful tool requiring full management understanding and support. The results are well worth the effort.

Selected References

Gainsharing

Anonymous. (December 5, 2002). "Debates to Start on Changes to Productivity Act of 1999." *Business World*. Pg. 2

Anonymous. (May 29, 2002). "IPMA Benchmarking Surveys Offer Insights Into Best Practices." *Managing Today's Federal Employees*. 3(12).

Anonymous. (October 2001). "How the U.S. Mint has Profited from Gainsharing." *IOMA Pay for Performance Report*. Pg. 1

Anonymous. (September 28, 2001). "Local Firm Finds Cash King Among Worker Incentives." *Business First*. 18(5):B11.

Beatty, Richard W., Ph.D. (October 2000). "Making the Connection Between Performance and Pay." *workspan*. 43(10):78.

Lesieur, Fredrick G. (1958). *The Scanlon Plan: A Frontier in Labor-Management Cooperation*. The MIT Press.

Masternak, Robert. L. (Winter 1991-92). "Gainsharing Programs at Two Fortune 500 Facilities: Why One Worked Better." *National Productivity Review*.

Masternak, Robert. L. (Winter 1993-94). "Gainsharing: Overcoming Common Myths and Problems to Achieve Dramatic Results." *Employee Relations Today*.

Masternak, Robert. L. (Spring 1993). "Gainsharing Boosts Quality and Productivity at a BFGoodrich Plant." *National Productivity Review*.

Masternak, Robert. L. (September/October 1997). "How to Make Gainsharing Successful: The Collective Experience of 17 Facilities." *Compensation & Benefits Review*, September/October 1997.

McAdams, Jerry L., CCP, and Hawk, Elizabeth J., CCP. (Third Quarter 2000). "Making Group Incentive Plans Work." *WorldatWork Journal*. 9(3):28-34.

McAdams, Jerry L., and Hawk, Elizabeth J., CCP. (1992). *Capitalizing on Human Assets*. American Compensation Association.

Milkovich, George T., and Newman, Jerry M. (2001). "Compensation (Seventh Edition)." McGraw Hill. Book. ISBN 0-07243-6719.

Paulsen, Kevin, and Westman, David. (July/August 1999). "Using Gainsharing to Motivate Generation X." *ACA News*. 42(7):44-48.

Reissman, Larry. (May 2001). "Keeping Line-of-Sight in Perspective — During Incentive Plan Design." *workspan*. 44(5):78-82.

Remmen, Doreen. (March 1, 2003). "Performance Pays Off." *Strategic Finance*. 84(9):27.

Risher, Howard, Ph.D. (March 1999). "Viewpoint: Changing Compensation Beliefs." *ACA News*. 42(3):6-8.

Shives, Gregory K., and Scott, Dow K., Ph.D. (First Quarter 2003). "Gainsharing and EVA, the U.S. Postal Service Experience." *WorldatWorkJournal*. 12(1):21-30.

Incentive Compensation

Anonymous. (July 2001). "What is My Motivation?" *Call Center Magazine*. 14(7):118-120.

Cadrain, Diane. (May 1, 2003). "Put Success in Sight: Show Employees the Link Between Their Jobs and Company Goals." *HRMagazine*. 48(5):84.

Ferracone, Robin A. (Autumn 2001). "Putting Pay for Performance Back Into Incentive Programs." *Compensation & Benefits Management*. 17(4):29-35.

Friedman, Lori, and St. Ville, Thomas J. (December 1, 2002). "Pay Me Later Please: Looking for Ways to Boost Your Post-Association Income?" *Association Management*. 54(13):51.

Hutson, Darryl A. (March/April 2002). "Shopping for Incentives." *Compensation and Benefits Review*. 34(2):75-79.

Jensen, Michael C. (November 2001). "Corporate Budgeting is Broken—Let's Fix it." *Harvard Business Review*. Pg. 94.

Kurlander, Peter. (July/August 2001). "Building Incentive Compensation Management Systems: What Can Go Wrong?" *Compensation and Benefits Review*. 33(4):52-56.

Liccione, William J. (March/April 2002). "Plan Design and Work/Life Management in Incentive Compensation." *Compensation and Benefits Review*. 34(2):41-48.

Lyons, Frank H. (March/April 2002). "Total Rewards Strategy: The Best Foundation of Pay for Performance." *Compensation and Benefits Review*. 34(2):34-40.

Marks, Susan J. (June 2001). "Incentives That Really Reward and Motivate." *Workforce.* 80(6):108-114.

National Center for Employee Ownership. (May 1999). *Incentive Compensation and Employee Ownership, Third Edition.* NCEO. ISBN 0-926902-54-7.

Olson, Scott, and Jesuthasan, Ravin. (November 1, 2002). "Pay-to-Stay Incentives in Winning Deals." *Mergers and Acquisitions Journal.*

Perlmutter, Andrew L. (March/April 2002). "Taking Motivation and Recognition Online." *Compensation and Benefits Review.* 34(2):70-74.

Renn, Robert W., Ph.D.; Van Scotter, James R., Ph.D.; Barksdale, W. Kevin, Ph.D., and Hutton, Chuck. (July/August 2001). *Compensation and Benefits Review.* 33(4):68-73.

Satterfield, Brian. (Third Quarter 2002). "Evaluating Long-Term Incentive Alternatives." *Benefits Quarterly.* 18(3):17-21.

Scharff, Robert L. Jr. (Autumn 2001). "Viewpoint: Companies Need Holistic Strategies and Incentives to Attract and Retain Key Executives." *Compensation & Benefits Management.* 17(4):58-60.

Thompson, Elizabeth D. (April 2003). "Motivating Employees." *Credit Union Magazine.* 46(4):56-60.

Turnasella, Ted. (March/April 2002). "Pay and Personality." *Compensation and Benefits Review.* 34(2):49-59.

Uyl, Janet Den. (September 2002). "Executive Benefits in a Pay-for-Performance Environment." *Employee Benefits Journal.* 27(3):14-22.

Rewards

Batutis, Susan. (August 2002). "Money Talks for Northeastern University Employees." *workspan.* 45(8):44-47.

Brown, Duncan. (Third Quarter 2001). "Rewards Strategies for Real: Moving from Intent to Impact." *WorldatWork Journal.* 10(3):42-49.

Crandall, N. Fredric. (February 1999). "An Explanation of Rewards in the Virtual Workplace." *Workforce.* Workforce Extra: 6-7.

Fuller, Jeffrey J., and Tinkham, Rebecca. (September 2002). "Making the Most Scarce Reward Dollars: Why Differentiation Makes a Difference." *Employee Benefits Journal*. 27(3):3-7.

Gherson, Diane J. (June 2000). "Getting the Pay Thing Right." *workspan*. 43(6):47-51.

Handel, Jeremy. (August 2000). "It's All About People." *workspan*. 43(8):50-51.

Ledford, Gerry, Ph.D.; Mulvey, Paul, Ph.D., and LeBlanc, Peter, CCP. (2000). *The Rewards of Work: What Employees Value*. WorldatWork. ISBN: 1-57963-0812.

Mulvey, Paul W., Ph.D.; Ledford, Gerald E., Ph.D., and LeBlanc, Peter V., CCP. (Third Quarter 2000). "Rewards of Work, How They Drive Performance, Retention and Satisfaction." *WorldatWork Journal*. 9(3):6-18.

Outram, Jake, and Gilbert, Tony. (January 2003). "Six Key Practices to Link Rewards to Long-Term Financial Success." *workspan*. 46(1):32-35.

Parus, Barbara. (February 1999). "Designing a Total Rewards Program to Retain Critical Talent in the New Millennium." *ACA News*. 42(2):20-23.

Pfau, Bruce N., Ph.D., and Kay, Ira T., Ph.D. (Third Quarter 2002). "The Five Key Elements of a Total Rewards and Accountability Orientation." *Benefits Quarterly*. 18(3):7-15.

Plachy, Roger, and Plachy, Sandra. (May/June 1999). "Rewarding Employees Who Truly Make a Difference." *Compensation and Benefits Review*. 31(3):34-39.

Puffer, Sheila M. (May 1999). "CompUSA's CEO James Halpin on Technology, Rewards and Commitment." *The Academy of Management Executive*. 13(2):29-36.

Sanders, Debbie. (First Quarter 2001). "Beyond Face Value — Painting the Total Rewards Portrait." *WorldatWork Journal*. 10(1):63-69.

WorldatWork. (2000). *Total Rewards: From Strategy to Implementation, a Total Rewards Guidebook*. WorldatWork. ISBN: 1-57963-0820.

Young, Marjorie, M.Ed., MPA, and Roach, John, Ph.D. (May 2003). "Accentuate the Positives." *workspan*. 46(5):50-52.

Zingheim, Patricia K., Ph.D., and Schuster, Jay R., Ph.D. (May 2003). "Getting Back to Basics." *workspan*. 46(5):54-58.

Zingheim, Patricia K., Ph.D., and Schuster, Jay R., Ph.D. (May 2002). "Aligning Total Rewards for Global Economic Recovery." *workspan*. 45(5):20-26.

Zingheim, Patricia K., Ph.D., and Schuster Jay R., Ph.D. (Second Quarter 2000). "Pay People Right! Book Excerpt." *WorldatWork Journal*. 9(2):42-50.

Zingheim, Patricia K., Ph.D., and Schuster Jay R., Ph.D. (2000). *Pay People Right: Breakthrough Reward Strategies to Create Great Companies*. Jossey-Bass. ISBN: 0-7879-4016-X.